RECEIVED

OCT 09 2018

BROADVIEW LIBRARY

NO LONGER PROPERTY OF
SEATTLE PUBLIC LIBRARY

Paddling the

JOHN WESLEY POWELL ROUTE

D0796862

Packrafting the Colorado River in Glen Canyon while searching for a loop from Lee's Ferry.

Paddling the

JOHN WESLEY POWELL ROUTE

Exploring the Green and Colorado Rivers

MIKE BEZEMEK

FALCON®

Guilford, Connecticut

FALCON®

An imprint of The Rowman & Littlefield Publishing Group, Inc.
4501 Forbes Blvd., Ste. 200
Lanham, MD 20706
www.rowman.com

Falcon and FalconGuides are registered trademarks and Make Adventure Your Story is a trademark of The Rowman & Littlefield Publishing Group, Inc.

Distributed by NATIONAL BOOK NETWORK

Copyright © 2018 Mike Bezemek

All photos by Mike Bezemek unless otherwise noted

Maps © The Rowman & Littlefield Publishing Group, Inc.

All rights reserved. No part of this book may be reproduced in any form or by any electronic or mechanical means, including information storage and retrieval systems, without written permission from the publisher, except by a reviewer who may quote passages in a review.

British Library Cataloguing-in-Publication Information available

Library of Congress Cataloging-in-Publication Data available

ISBN 978-1-4930-3481-9 (paperback)
ISBN 978-1-4930-3482-6 (e-book)

∞™ The paper used in this publication meets the minimum requirements of American National Standard for Information Sciences—Permanence of Paper for Printed Library Materials, ANSI/NISO Z39.48-1992.

Printed in the United States of America

The authors and The Rowman & Littlefield Publishing Group, Inc. assume no liability for accidents happening to, or injuries sustained by, readers who engage in the activities described in this book.

For the boaters who showed me how. For the boaters I've met along the way.
And for the boaters we've lost but still float with us through these canyons.

Last rays from a setting
sun illuminate a butte in
Desolation Canyon on the
Green River.

Contents

0. Upper Green River and Lakes   1

Upstream of the Powell route, paddle beneath the dramatic Wind River Range or through a peaceful wildlife refuge.

- State-by-State Watercraft Regulations

- Name That River: The Green, the Colorado—and the Grand?

- Prologue: "All" of History Before 1869, with Apologies, in Seven Paragraphs

1. Flaming Gorge Reservoir   19

From Expedition Island to a surreal desert reservoir, the first "official" segment offers everything from easy day trips to a 90-mile proving ground for through-paddlers.

- Outfitters, Services, and Supplies for Flaming Gorge Country and Red Canyon

- Who Starts from an Island?

- 1869, Part I: Those Early, Carefree Days Near Flaming Gorge

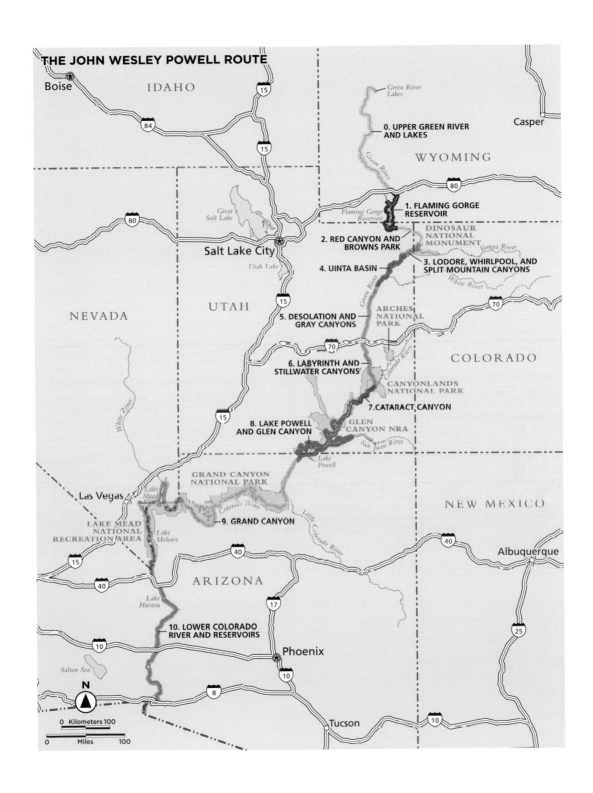

THE JOHN WESLEY POWELL ROUTE

Boise

IDAHO

Casper

Green River Lakes

0. UPPER GREEN RIVER AND LAKES

WYOMING

Green River

Great Salt Lake

Flaming Gorge Reservoir

1. FLAMING GORGE RESERVOIR

Salt Lake City

Utah Lake

2. RED CANYON AND BROWNS PARK

DINOSAUR NATIONAL MONUMENT

Yampa River

4. UINTA BASIN

3. LODORE, WHIRLPOOL, AND SPLIT MOUNTAIN CANYONS

White River

UTAH

NEVADA

Green River

ARCHES NATIONAL PARK

5. DESOLATION AND GRAY CANYONS

COLORADO

Colorado River

6. LABYRINTH AND STILLWATER CANYONS

CANYONLANDS NATIONAL PARK

7. CATARACT CANYON

White River

8. LAKE POWELL AND GLEN CANYON

GLEN CANYON NRA

San Juan River

Lake Powell

GRAND CANYON NATIONAL PARK

Las Vegas

Lake Mead

NEW MEXICO

LAKE MEAD NATIONAL RECREATION AREA

Lake Mohave

Colorado River

9. GRAND CANYON

Little Colorado River

Albuquerque

ARIZONA

Lake Havasu

10. LOWER COLORADO RIVER AND RESERVOIRS

Phoenix

Salton Sea

N

Tucson

0 Kilometers 100

0 Miles 100

Foreword:
Welcome to the Powell Route!

Imagine you're in the Gates of Lodore, standing on shore as the scout for Hell's Half Mile, and a kayaker turns to you and says, "Moldy flour." Or envision yourself floating through Labyrinth Canyon when a passing canoeist drops the phrase "rancid bacon." Or suppose you're rowing nervously for your first time into Hance Rapids in the Grand Canyon when a gawker on shore shouts, "Protect the coffee!" Would you grasp the references?

If such phrases hold meaning for many Western boaters today, it's all due to the sorry state of John Wesley Powell's rations during his 1869 expedition. The challenges he and his group faced have become as much a part of modern river lore as the image of Powell himself—the one-armed Civil War veteran sitting in an armchair lashed to the deck of a wooden boat, barking orders at his ragtag crew of mountain men.

Powell's daring 1,000-mile journey down the Green and Colorado Rivers has lodged in our collective memory in part because of the danger and adventure and in part because it colored in the last major blank spot on the American map, back when the West was still wild. But Powell's story has stuck with us also because most of the canyons he explored have changed little in the century and a half since he first floated them. Sure, the country's two largest reservoirs, Lake Mead and his namesake Lake Powell, now cover portions of the route. And there are a few bridges scattered here and there. But the John Wesley Powell route still offers one of the greatest opportunities for wilderness river adventure on the planet.

I know this because in 2011, Will Stauffer-Norris and I, both fresh out of college and looking to paddle away from the looming threat of careers, traversed the entirety of Powell's route by going source to sea on the Green and Colorado Rivers. We completed the journey in the off-season months of October to December. During our whole trip, we saw no other overnight boaters outside of the Grand Canyon (so, yeah, maybe that *was* me shouting about coffee at Hance). Sometimes we paddled 20 miles apart for days on end just to soak up the solitude.

During one such solo paddle through Desolation Canyon, I remember how the river glowed golden as I pulled into camp for the evening. I stepped out of my kayak onto a beach that didn't have a single human footprint. What lay in the sand, instead, were mountain lion tracks, hundreds of them, marking where the cat had recently paced along the river before bedding down beneath a cottonwood. The day was late,

Scouting class IV Hance Rapid in Grand Canyon (about 775 paddling miles from Green River, WY) has caused numerous "dry gulps."

and frost was already forming on my PFD, so I unrolled my sleeping bag. As the stars began to pierce the sky, the canyons seemed just as wild as they'd been in Powell's day.

Employment eventually found me. I became an editor for *Canoe & Kayak* magazine. One of the best parts of the job is working with a talented writer named Mike Bezemek, who pens the columns *Regular Paddler, Remarkable Waters*, and *Weekend Expeditions*. Mike's writing is superb. His articles always feature engaging storylines, crisp descriptions, careful research, and gentle humor. More than anything else, though, I like working with Mike because his passion for paddling is apparent in every paragraph. Whether he's recounting his line in a class V rapid or recalling a leisurely weekend float, his love of rivers is infectious.

So, when Mike told me his next project was writing a book about the Powell route, I was thrilled. My favorite guidebook author, who previously wrote *Paddling the Ozarks*, would be bringing his talents to my favorite 1,000-plus miles of river.

This book lives up to all my expectations. Not only does the book present invaluable technical information that is clear, concise, and extensively field-checked, but it is also a joy to read, thanks to a colorful historical retelling and lively sidebars. Like all good river guides, Mike and his book will take you to the river by day and will entertain you by the fire each night.

In the quote below, taken from Powell's account of the expedition, he describes floating through the Grand Canyon in August 1869, full of uncertainty about what waited downstream. A century and a half later, one thing is certain. With *Paddling the John Wesley Powell Route* as your guide, the sense of adventure from the original expeditions will accompany you on every trip through the canyons he named.

"WE ARE NOW READY TO START ON OUR WAY DOWN THE GREAT UNKNOWN. . . . WE ARE THREE QUARTERS OF A MILE INTO THE DEPTHS OF THE EARTH, AND THE GREAT RIVER SHRINKS INTO INSIGNIFICANCE AS IT DASHES ITS ANGRY WAVES AGAINST THE WALLS AND CLIFFS THAT RISE TO THE WORLD ABOVE. . . . WE HAVE AN UNKNOWN DISTANCE YET TO RUN, AN UNKNOWN RIVER TO EXPLORE. WHAT FALLS THERE ARE, WE KNOW NOT; WHAT ROCKS BESET THE CHANNEL, WE KNOW NOT; WHAT WALLS RISE OVER THE RIVER, WE KNOW NOT. AH, WELL! WE MAY CONJECTURE MANY THINGS."

—*John Wesley Powell*

Zak Podmore is an editor-at-large for *Canoe & Kayak* magazine. In 2011–12, he paddled the Green and Colorado Rivers from their headwaters toward the Gulf of California but had to hike the final 90 miles. In 2014, he returned during the "pulse flow" water release and witnessed the Colorado reconnect with the sea for the first time in decades. He's also paddled a flash flood down the Little Colorado River to examine recent attempts to build a tramway into the Grand Canyon. Read these stories and more at canoekayak.com. Zak lives in southern Utah, where he's at work on his first book.

Acknowledgments

To begin, I feel compelled to honor the essential contributions of liquid water. Water, you've been there the entire way—all 5 years and thousands of river miles I spent on the project that became this book and much, much longer. Like *billions* of years longer. Just doing what you do, in a most fantastic desert, so we can do what we do with boats. You're the best, water.

Next, a major thanks to all the boaters who participated in our first "fresh eyes" descents, including Paul Polewaczyk, Curtis Ahlers, Rick Neal, Nicky Neal, Amanda Lappe, Brad Moschetti, Courtney Hart, Dan Macheca, Mitch Wieldt, Sam Bania, Kelly Kastens, Will Scherff, Sam Scherff, Di McHenry, Chuck McHenry, Nate Howard, and my wife, Ina Seethaler. Plus, a huge thanks to all the boaters I met along the way or did subsequent trips with. Many of you offered gracious help and welcome information. I am lucky to have become friends with so many cool people.

I'd like to offer a big thanks to Zak Podmore for writing the foreword and reviewing the manuscript—along with Dave Shively and Jeff Moag, all three of *Canoe & Kayak* magazine—for supporting my work these many years. Thank you, David Legere, Melissa Baker, and the team at Falcon for editing and producing this book and the last one. And thank you to the many fantastic contributors and companies who provided vital photos, interviews, information, contacts, books, journals, materials, logistics, shuttles, equipment, and one very welcome high-water rescue: Justin Baile, Jonathan Bowler, Sinjin Eberle, Max Gans and the 2017 CAT crew at Sherri Griffith Expeditions, Lars Haan and OARS, Peter Holcombe, Nate Howard, James Kaiser, Mick Krussow, Brendan Leonard, Amy Martin, Tom Minckley, Hilary Oliver, Kirk Rasmussen and NOLS, Will Stauffer-Norris, Whit Richardson, Doc Searls, and Forest Woodward.

Thank you to the outfitters who helped with logistics—Dutch John Resort, River Runners Transport, Canyon REO, and Desert River Outfitters. Thank you to the US Geologic Survey and Grand Canyon National Park for their Powell Expedition photo collections. Thank you to historians Tim Glenn at the JW Powell River History Museum in Green River, Mark Law at the Powell Museum in Page, and Dave Mead at Sweetwater County Museum; and thanks to Michael Ghiglieri for expertly compiling the original journal accounts in *First Through Grand Canyon*. Plus, other great guidebook authors whose work I've used for years, including the Belknaps and Tom Martin. Anyone remember *Western Whitewater*?! —shout-out to the original classic.

Seeing the underside of Navajo Bridge, just downstream from Lees Ferry, means one thing: Grand Canyon trip!

Also, a big belated thank-you—I'm always running about 150 years behind on stuff—to the original ten expedition members, without whom people might say to me, "So you wrote a fictional guidebook? That's weird." Anyway, I appreciate the memories, John Wesley Powell, George Bradley, Jack Sumner, Oramel Howland, Andy Hall, Billy Hawkins, Bill Dunn, Walter Powell, Seneca Howland, and Frank Goodman. Plus, nice work, members of the second expedition, especially Frederick Dellenbaugh, Almon Harris Thompson, E. O. Beaman, and J. K. Hillers.

And two final mentions to a pair of natural phenomena. First, the sun. Yeah, the one up in the sky. You can be pretty harsh at times, but you're absolutely amazing when I stop to think about it. The Mayans definitely had some stuff figured out. What you've done out in the canyons of the Southwest is beyond words, beyond photos, beyond imagination. But, of course, none of it could have happened without geology. Yes, technically, water did most of the recent work, but let's not split atoms here. Geology, without you, we'd have no rapids, no downstream currents, no excuses to dress up like postapocalyptic superheroes with terrible color coordination who hoot and holler between splashes. Geology, without you, people would think paddlers are just strange cult members who stare at cliffs from boats—okay, that's fair, actually. Geology, without you, we river runners would probably have more stable jobs. Take a bow, geology. But please be careful. You're looking kind of friable these days. And with that river-runner knee slap, let's get on with it . . .

Introduction

On May 24, 1869, John Wesley Powell and nine crewmen in four wooden rowboats set off down the Green River from the town of Green River Station, WY. Powell was a retired US Army major turned self-taught professor, who lost his right arm at the Battle of Shiloh. The goal of his geographic expedition was to fill the last "blank spot" on the map of the United States, particularly the inconsistent plotting of the Colorado River through the little-explored Grand Canyon. Wild rumors reported plunging waterfalls or the river simply vanishing into the bowels of the earth. You know, big-time hero stuff.

Secured in the hatches of their wooden-keeled boats, the expedition members carried rations, equipment, and clothing expected to last 10 months. They planned to map the route and adjacent topography, holing up through the winter if necessary. Although some of the men had experience with boats on lakes and flatwater rivers, none had whitewater experience. It just wasn't a thing back then. What could possibly go wrong?

This relief mural by Franz Johansen—outside the J. W. Powell River History Museum in Green River, UT—gets my vote for finest use of cement along the route. Honorable mention to the building foundation of Phantom Ranch Canteen, where you can have a cold beer in Upper Granite Gorge during summer.

Three months later, six men in two boats emerged from the Grand Canyon of the Colorado River near the Grand Wash Cliffs. Not unlike modern river runners ending a 3-week canyon trip, these guys stank to high heaven, and their clothes looked more like rags. But that is where the similarity ends. And what happened along the 1,000 river miles in between quickly became the stuff of legend. The story of the 1869 Powell expedition still captures the imaginations of modern river runners in the form of riverside retellings and armchair readings. But the accepted facts surrounding that first expedition continue to evolve in scope and complexity through reexaminations by scholars and historians.

A few things we do know are that one man left the expedition in the Uinta Basin, while three others left a few days before the end. Those three men were never seen again—presumed murdered in a convoluted story presented in my multipart retelling. When the remaining six men reached the mouth of the Virgin River, they were exhausted and near starving. And the expedition had basically failed in all but one objective. Along with one boat lost in the Canyon of Lodore, the instruments were mostly destroyed. The observations and maps were either lost or incomplete. What survived were some remarkable personal journals and proof that the entire route, including the Colorado River through the Grand Canyon, could be descended by boats—just with great difficulty and an obscene amount of portaging. Sound like fun? Okay, let's go!

Well, that's kind of what happened. Though not in great numbers. By 1950, river historian Dock Marsten reported that only 100 small groups and individuals had boated through the Grand Canyon. The first to return was Powell, with a more methodical scientific expedition that involved a new crew and plenty of land-based surveying but the river running stopped short at Kanab Creek due to high water. Next came a disastrous expedition hoping to build a railroad through the

A portrait of John Wesley Powell around 1869, when he was 35 years old and going through a facial hair "experimentation" phase. NATIONAL PARK SERVICE

canyon. More wooden boats followed, but the techniques and equipment evolved. Soon rowers faced downstream and were running more and more rapids. Next, rubber rafts, surplus from World War II, became the craft of choice along the whitewater sections of the entire Powell route. Kayaks grew in popularity, as did dories, canoes, packrafts, and recently paddleboards, though mostly along the flatwater sections. Eventually, every rapid along the route was run regularly.

Today, the John Wesley Powell route is a very different place than it was 150 years ago. Vast segments are protected by various agencies, including the National Park Service, US Forest Service, Bureau of Land Management (BLM), and Native American reservations. Three major dams and reservoirs have flooded about 40 percent of the route, resulting in scorn from river lovers but plenty of lake paddling for those interested. On the remaining river segments, tens of thousands of boaters annually descend many beloved and permitted sections, some requiring advance lottery applications. Meanwhile, many sections remain unpermitted or require self-issued permits, while other sections are rarely paddled and seem almost forgotten. The result is plenty of remarkable paddling opportunities existing within a complex network of interwoven agencies and regulations.

Luckily, one thing hasn't changed. The John Wesley Powell route still offers some of the most unique and adventurous paddling in the United States. This book provides an overview of the paddling and exploring opportunities along that route, plus a few adjacent segments, including practical and logistical information about the many sections. A series of linked sidebars shares the history of the 1869 expedition, while other sidebars explore relevant topics, and there are a few interviews with modern explorers. There are photos and overview maps to help visualize the route. And resource sections direct interested parties toward outfitters, services, and relevant materials—including further reading and topographic maps.

This book covers the entire Green River and two-thirds of the Colorado River across six states, including Wyoming, Utah, Colorado, Arizona, Nevada, and California. Paddlers will find the perfect adventures to fit their abilities, interests, and time frames—from just a few hours to even a few months. Weekend canoe trips past the buttes and cliffs of Canyonlands National Park. Whitewater rafting through crashing waves in Cataract Canyon or beneath a billion years of twisted geology in Dinosaur National Monument. Peaceful floats through high desert valleys and wildlife refuges in Browns Park or the Uinta Basin. Paddleboarding into little-known coves and bays on reservoirs like Flaming Gorge or Lake Powell. Afternoon kayaking amid the rapids of Red Canyon or week-long expeditions through the surprising scenery of Desolation Canyon. Plus, the *original trip of a lifetime* down the Grand Canyon.

Along the way, enjoy side hikes to preserved ruins, ancient petroglyphs, historic sites, and unexpected waterfalls. Watch herds of bighorn sheep trot along cliffs lined

> "DOWN IN THESE GRAND, GLOOMY DEPTHS WE GLIDE, EVER LISTENING, FOR THE MAD WATERS KEEP UP THEIR ROAR; EVER WATCHING, EVER PEERING AHEAD, FOR THE NARROW CANYON IS WINDING AND THE RIVER IS CLOSED IN SO THAT WE CAN SEE BUT A FEW HUNDRED YARDS, AND WHAT THERE MAY BE BELOW WE KNOW NOT; SO WE LISTEN FOR FALLS AND WATCH FOR ROCKS, STOPPING NOW AND THEN IN THE BAY OF A RECESS TO ADMIRE THE GIGANTIC SCENERY...."
>
> —*John Wesley Powell*

by barrel cactuses. Follow bald eagles soaring over craggy outcrops and scrubby cedar. Stare into unbelievable starry nights that spread above towering rock temples. With this book as your guide, come explore the same sections of the Green and Colorado Rivers as the original expedition—and learn firsthand about one of the greatest adventure stories in American history.

THE MANY PATHS TO BECOMING A POWELL ROUTE "PILGRIM"

My first visit to the Grand Canyon was a week-long guided backpacking trip after freshman year at UC Davis. Camped at Hance, I watched rafts and kayaks navigate the rapid with hoots and hollers. I thought, *Man, I want to do that.* Luckily, Outdoor Adventures at UCD offered a whitewater guide school. A year later, I was a raft guide and beginning kayaker. I expected to return and paddle or row the canyon within another year or two.

But that fall, while guiding, I twisted my back kind of funny. Then, while hiking on the volcano Stromboli in the Tyrrhenian Sea—long

The 6-cent (Six cents! No wonder the post office went broke!) postage stamp was released in 1969 to commemorate the 100th anniversary of the first Powell expedition.

story—I slipped while descending and ruptured a disc in my spine. At 20 years old, my hopes of becoming a fulltime class V guide and kayaker seemed dashed. While I did incrementally return to paddling over the following years, physical limitations meant I missed a lot. Just tucking up for a roll sent stabbing pain down my sciatic nerve—still hurts but less so.

Since I couldn't row or sit comfortably in a kayak for many years, I declined in-state creeks, out-of-state multidays, even expeditions to other countries. Worst of all was saying no to the Grand. I turned away private trips, an offer to row a gear boat on a geology field trip, and an opportunity to swamp and maybe progress to becoming a commercial guide. Eventually, the offers stopped. I left California for grad school in St. Louis, where I focused on writing, teaching, and daytrip whitewater kayaking in the Ozarks and Southeast.

Years passed, and the Canyon lurked in my mind but felt distant and out of reach. Sure, I could try to fish out an invite to a private trip with an established group through my paddling network. But to me—bad pun—that ship had sailed. Many of those groups were on their third, fourth, or fifth Canyon trips by now. And I'd heard the way the talk changed as trips in the Canyon or along the Powell route piled up for veterans. The first trips had a surreal and mythical quality, which soon gave way to a crusty all-knowing attitude, a sort of do-this, don't-do-that, this-is-best, that's-overrated kind of thing. This felt like salt to my spinal injury. I didn't want to follow veterans down the river and see it through their eyes. I wanted that feeling of awe my friends had described from their first trips, that fresh-eyed excitement that comes with exploring the personally unknown.

So instead, I bided my time, kept on kayaking, and held on to my extra chances after transitioning from the old waiting list. Eventually, I shared my idea with some great friends who were excellent boaters from St. Louis and the Ozarks. I suggested a fresh-eyes descent, meaning none of us in the group had ever boated the river before. For the Grand Canyon, we'd go in winter, when permits are easier to pull and almost no one else is down there. We'd get our own exploratory expedition—sort of like Powell. So I entered the lottery, and we won a December launch for 20 months ahead.

But before we went, I had a major realization. *Like Powell*, I'd said. Here was a figure I thought of as a hero of mine. We Californian raft guides often talked about Powell with the reverence usually reserved for saints or whoever started In-N-Out Burger. But I knew almost nothing beyond the basics. Powell's team first boated the canyon in 1869, and the crews rowed backward—a few details all reported on a postage stamp! So I started reading. Book after book. Journals, histories, opinions, trip reports. Powell, Dellenbaugh, Stegner, Stanton, Ghiglieri, Dolnick, Zwinger, Belknap, Martin, Fedarko.

My head was swimming. There were two expeditions? Powell embellished or maybe lied? The three who left may have been killed by Mormons who blamed local Shivwits tribesmen? I decided a single Grand trip would not suffice. Like many paddlers, I became infatuated with one of the greatest adventure stories in US history. I wanted to follow Powell's entire expedition route, which grew in reverence with each new fact I learned, and each controversy I discovered only deepened the mystery. I wanted to be a Powell route pilgrim.

So that's what I did but not as I had first hoped. I briefly considered taking a semester off from adjunct teaching, but I dropped that notion due to financial realities. Then I tried to go in segments in order, but I couldn't get the permits to line up with my time off. Instead, I settled on doing the route in segments, over several years, in whatever order was possible. And I did them all as fresh-eyes descents. Usually, I did these trips with a few friends in small groups, while a few hundred miles were solo by kayak or oar raft. So as not to miss anything along the way, we did extensive research and preparation. After those first trips, I kept returning to the route, joining veterans' river trips, chatting with route aficionados, and following many portions alongshore—hiking, biking, and driving—to gain those perspectives, as well.

At times, the fresh-eyes approach created unique challenges and hilarious mistakes, which I share in a few sidebars plus external articles and blog posts that can be reached via my website, mikebezemek.com. At other times, the outsider perspective allowed me to learn things I might never have discovered otherwise. By accident, I stumbled across the actual starting location of at least Powell's second expedition and probably his first. I learned that a tale I'd been told my entire paddling career, about a trade of one dam for another, never happened. And I began to question if Powell really was the hero he was thought to be—or if that even matters. This book is essentially my report on those explorations, supplemented by input from essential contributors. This was my path to becoming a Powell route pilgrim, and I hope this book will help readers find their own paths to exploring this unique and remarkable paddling route.

TYPES OF TRIPS

There's no right way to experience the Powell route, but there is one wrong way—and that's not to experience it at all. Below are a few drastically different approaches, from the easy to the challenging. Once you know your desired method, proceed to the Trip Finder and Resources chapters to start planning!

Day trips. The Powell route is best known for classic multiday expeditions, but there are actually dozens of one-day opportunities. Flatwater half days through wildlife refuges, full-day whitewater adventures through lofty gorges, and open-water out-and-backs on reservoirs.

Student Tim Johns digs in during a NOLS whitewater paddling school along the Powell route. For more great adventure photography by Kirk Rasmussen, check out www.topo-media.com! KIRK RASMUSSEN/NOLS

Guided trips and courses. There are dozens of great outfitters offering countless guided trips along the route. To learn more, check out the interview with OARS guide Lars Haarr on page xlvii. Learn about special opportunities, such as Powell-themed trips by Sherri Griffith Expeditions, and paddling schools operating on the route, like NOLS, on page xlii. Plus, find listings for specific companies and offerings within the segments.

Overnight trips. Not all multiday trips along the route require a week or more on the water. Many DIY 2-day or 3-day trips, perfect for a weekend adventure, can be found in the segments. Some are well known, while others have almost been forgotten due to remoteness or inattention.

Multisport and vehicle trips. Certain portions of the Powell route are particularly suited for exploration by foot, bike, car, motorboat, and pack animal. You'll need to conduct supplementary research, but I point out a few opportunities within the segments.

Multiday trips. The Powell route contains some of the best multiday river trips in the country—but you'll need advance permits for many classic sections.

Through-paddling. This book is organized into eleven segments, many of which are composed of several shorter sections that can be combined into longer trips. I use the term *through-paddling* to indicate trips that span an entire segment or combine sections or segments into a longer trip.

Source-to-sea. These are the passion of long-distance paddlers who have a soft spot for pain. Going from the headwaters of the Green River in the Wind River Range to the Colorado River and then onward to the Gulf of California includes the entire 1,000-mile Powell route, plus 200 miles above and 500 miles below. If you ever meet paddlers attempting this 1,700-mile odyssey, buy them a beer and some clean underwear—they probably need it.

WHAT TO EXPECT ALONG THE ROUTE

With this book spanning about 1,600 river miles across six states, summing up the Powell route is about as easy as writing a chapter on *what to expect as a parent* for a book about not ruining your kid. What can you expect along the Powell route? Other than humidity, almost anything.

Landscape. One of the biggest pulls of the Powell route is the scenery. At first glance, it might seem as though it's all just one big desert, but the variety across the route is surprising: high-elevation canyons where pines and firs cling to rocky crags, open basins where every cactus seems cockier than a raft guide, sandy bottomlands where green oases pop up from rugged alcoves like Butch and Sundance running from the law, and deep gorges that rise with confusing and breathtaking complexity. Just saying, consider bringing a camera.

Geology. The reason for such startling canyon landscapes—plus, why the official "blank spot" remained for so long on the US map—is related to one major and many smaller geologic events. The major event is the Laramide orogeny, named for the Laramie Mountains, located about 200 miles east of Green River, WY. From a paddling perspective, this event created two of the three major geologic regions paddlers will encounter along the Powell route. Roughly 75 million to 45 million years ago, oceanic crust subducted at a low angle underneath the North American continent, causing a period of mountain building and crustal deformation, specifically shortening, in what is now the western United States. A common analogy is a rug being pushed across the floor, which bunches up into uneven bulges.

Expect a lot of paddling and slow-moving current along many ridiculously scenic sections of the Powell route. Here, the Green River just above Flaming Gorge Reservoir.

One result of the Laramide orogeny was a rising of the Rocky Mountains, including an offshoot now called the Uinta Mountains. This east-to-west range was the cause of the first major canyons encountered on the Powell route, starting with Flaming Gorge. Here, the Green River curiously turns into a mountain range and begins winding in and out of the Uintas, creating a series of rising and falling canyons, including Horseshoe, Kingfisher, Red, and Swallow Canyons. Powell rightfully recognized the river had superimposed on the landscape, remaining roughly in place by cutting down with erosion even as the terrain rose up around the river. Today, this is called *river antecedence*. Just below Browns Park, the Green River makes its dramatic final entrance to the Uinta Mountains at Gates of Lodore. From there the river winds through some particularly tortured folds into Echo Park, through Whirlpool Canyon, and finally Split Mountain. The result is Dinosaur National Monument, which has exposed rocks spanning about 1.2 billion years of earth history.

Below Split Mountain, the Green River enters the Uinta Basin, where begins the second major geologic unit along the route—the Colorado Plateau. Another result of the Laramide orogeny, the plateau is a massive block of mostly marine sedimentary rock, which essentially rose in one uniform piece, explaining why much of the Powell route has canyons with horizontally banded rocks. Shaped like a lima bean about 400 miles tall and 250 miles wide (sounds like a great menu plan for a river trip, huh?), the plateau's center is not far from Lees Ferry, about 100 miles west of Four Corners.

During the ice ages, a cooler and wetter climate caused the erosive episodes that led to the rugged canyons that were so impenetrable to official American explorations up until Powell's time, but which river runners regularly explore today. In the Uinta Basin, the Green River begins gradually cutting down into the Colorado Plateau, while flowing in a meandering but roughly southwestern or southern direction, through Desolation, Gray, and Stillwater Canyons. After that, the Colorado River continues through Cataract, Glen, and Marble Canyons before making another dramatic turn to the west.

Here is where paddlers will encounter the third major geologic region along the Powell route, the Grand Canyon. Described by Powell as the great unknown, it is the deepest, steepest, and most rugged segment of the route that his expeditions explored. Today that great unknown has become one of the most studied landscapes on the planet, and discussion is beyond the scope of this book. (Nor do I want to get trolled.) Luckily, there are countless books, websites, and documentaries dedicated to the subject. A great place to find them is the Grand Canyon Association's online store at grandcanyon.org.

Most of the major rock formations have long been identified, including sequences of limestones and sandstones deposited in a warm and shallow sea that once covered North America. These sedimentary rocks comprise most of the rise of the Grand Canyon's walls. Meanwhile, beneath the sedimentary rocks in the inner gorge, paddlers will encounter metamorphic and igneous rock formations—also called basement rocks, such as Vishnu schist and Zoroaster granite—which formed deep within the earth's interior and were uplifted over time. Another amazing feature is found in the downstream third of the canyon, where volcanic eruptions occurred during the past few million years and periodically dammed the river and collapsed (no big whoop).

A final point to impart is that while the rock sequences themselves are well known, the exact timing and method of the Grand Canyon's formation are unclear and constantly debated by scientists. Prevailing theories point to a geologically recent creation, within 10 million years, which involved uplifting, higher erosion during periods of wetter climate, and episodes of stream capture, meaning previously unconnected drainages rudely erode into one another, causing all types of chaos between geologic neighbors. Well! All right, now that your brain feels like hot rocks, you should probably go jump in the river.

Weather. Yeah, they got a bit of that out there. Sure, most of the time the route is pretty sunny and there isn't a lot of shade, so many boaters bring sun umbrellas, sun clothes, sunscreens, and massive sun hats that flop around like palm fronds. The air is ridiculously dry—like toss a wet shirt at a rock in summer and it's dry before it

One major change since Powell's time is there are now *a lot* of dams and reservoirs—including Flaming Gorge, Glen Canyon, and Hoover—along the route, which affect everything from river flows or lake levels to water temps, sediment deposition, and plant and animal life.

lands. (Bring lotion.) Precipitation ranges from pretty dry in the north (9 inches/year near Vernal) to "are-you-gonna-drink-that-backwash?" in the south (6 inches/year in Grand Canyon).

When weather does strike, though, it often comes in powerful, even violent, bursts. Many of the canyon rims reach high into the sky, creating their own orographic effects. Thunderstorms are possible any time of year, while hail is always possible anywhere—plus snow, which is more common along the northern half of the route. Paddlers should prepare for winds, often coming up-canyon except during storms, when they might spiral in from anywhere. And oh, the sand! (Forehead clap.) It will work its way into everything—don't ever mention your relationship woes or retirement plans, because the sand will be in your face with an opinion. The Southwest monsoon season, affecting the lower two-thirds of the route, happens from mid-June to mid-September and often leads to afternoon thunderstorms. But just as sudden as any desert storm might rise—sometimes forming in minutes, often gathering for a few hours, occasionally lasting a few days—they will blow over, and the desert will unfold before you, quiet and empty, like nothing ever happened.

Flora. Plant life can be sparse but is always present along the way. At higher elevations and along the northern part of the route, expect more conifer forest. (For being called Red Canyon, it's pretty green with pines.) As the route continues south, canyon vegetation becomes increasingly scrubby, with more cedar and juniper. Eventually cactuses, such as yucca and barrel, come to dominate. Many unofficial and official campsites can be found nestled in bottomland pockets near a gigantic out-of-place tree called the cottonwood. These are different trees and not the same one following you down the river like a Tolkien Ent, haunting your every paddle stroke. Other common vegetation includes willows, which can provide some welcome and natural windbreaking in camp. Meanwhile, tamarisk, an invasive species being actively managed for reduction and removal, can make the shoreline in many sections almost impenetrable without bushwhacking.

Fauna. Wildlife is surprisingly abundant along the Powell route, and there are several national refuges along the way. There are bears in the northern part of the route, roughly Gray Canyon and upstream. There are some awesome jackrabbits, which look as though they are straight from a fantasy novel, in Flaming Gorge country. Some moose have ranged into northern Utah sections, but they're much easier to spot in Green River Valley (Segment 0). Bighorn sheep are in all of the canyons—a real highlight, especially when they hop from cliff to cliff or run along riverbanks in a herd. Antelope appear in the basins and valleys,

Prepare yourself for *a lot* of iconic vistas, like Horseshoe Bend in Glen Canyon. See the tiny river camps? They're about 690 paddling miles down the Powell route.

LEAVE-NO-TRACE PRINCIPLES FOR CAMPING AND BACKCOUNTRY TRAVEL

With the exception of established campgrounds and private property, much of the shore surrounding the river on the Powell route is public land. In the chapters, you'll find information on specific camping regulations required by managing agencies. Often these regulations are enhancements or variations on the seven principles of "leave no trace," which provide guidance for backcountry travels on how to limit human impact in order to preserve public lands for current and future visitors to enjoy. Here's a list adapted for the Powell route:

Plan and prepare by knowing all regulations, hazards, and conditions for where you're traveling (subtle plug for this book). Obtain a suitable map, and use a compass to properly orient yourself. Repackage food to minimize waste accumulation. You know, bring the right stuff.

Travel and camp on durable surfaces, such as sandbars, bedrock ledges, and previously established campsites instead of clearing the limited desert vegetation. Some rafters sleep on their floating boats—kayakers, I don't recommend trying this. Hike on existing trails or durable surfaces like sand, gravel, and bedrock. Avoid stepping on fragile macrobiotic soils, which are important to desert ecosystems and have a dark crust like black moss that takes a long time to rejuvenate.

Dispose of waste properly. In other words, pack it in, pack it out. Perform a sweep for trash before leaving your campsite. Don't create microtrash by tearing off little flecks of wrappers or scattering food crumbs, which lead to ant and rodent infestations. When a toilet system is not required, bury your feces in holes about 6 to 8 inches deep at least 200 feet from the river, creeks, camps, and trails. Where applicable, pack out used toilet paper and all other hygiene products. Urinate in the river (remember, precip is scarce and river runners use the same campsites night after night, which would smell like urinals, otherwise). Strain dishwater and dump in the river. Start getting used to strangers saying clever rhymes like "the solution to pollution is dilution."

Leave what you find. This is especially applicable on the Powell route. There are cultural artifacts, historic structures and ruins, rock art, artsy rocks, amazing cactuses. You name it, it's out there. Let's leave it out there. I mean, why carry around a bunch of heavy rocks, anyway? Please don't start carrying around a bunch of heavy rocks because I said that. You're better than that.

Minimize campfire impacts by using an appropriate firepan. In places where open fires are allowed, use existing fire rings. Put fires out at night so that a stiff wind doesn't burn down your camp like the Powell expeditions did twice. Pack your ashes out when required or dispose of them in the river where allowed.

Desert pavement, like this found in the White Rim section of Labyrinth Canyon, is a mysterious surface of uncertain formation.

Respect wildlife. I don't mean call the sheep mister, but at least keep your distance. Don't go stalking them like paparazzi, and don't feed them, because they'll get dependent and never leave your camp. Secure your food and trash properly so it doesn't end up all over the desert. Wildlife are like kids: Don't screw 'em up for life.

Be considerate of other visitors. Be courteous of adjacent campsites by not blasting your amazing waterproof speakers all night. Chat with fellow river travelers about overnight plans instead of racing them for camps—which is actually illegal in some managed sections. Don't be a put-in or take-out slob that dominates the ramp. Keep it tidy. In recent years, people have been vandalizing certain native and historic sites along the route. I don't even know what to say about that one. I'm speechless, and that's pretty rare for me.

For further discussion of flora, fauna, and more along the route, check out naturalist Anne Zwinger's books *Run, River, Run* and *Down Canyon, or A Naturalist's Guide to Canyon Country* by David Williams and Gloria Brown.

often called parks. Little critters onshore, such as deer mice and ringtail cats, are cute, hardy creatures known to chew through unattended backpacks and dry bags sniffing for snacks. Aquatic species include beaver, muskrat, and a variety of fish, including invasive species like carp, which often outcompete threatened native populations, like chub or pikeminnow, which are being actively managed for recovery. The tailwater sections below dams (Fontenelle, Flaming Gorge, Glen Canyon, and Hoover) are world-class trout fisheries. Birds include raptors like bald eagles and osprey, which sometimes territorially circle boating groups. Hawks, herons, ducks, geese, and so forth—there's a lot of sky out there. Ravens, particularly in Grand Canyon and other classic sections, are opportunists that snatch items—especially food—from your boats if you don't secure things during the night or while hiking.

Logistics. The transportation of river equipment to and from the river, the shuttling of vehicles between put-ins and take-outs, and the carrying of camping equipment and supplies during trips are some of the greatest challenges for excursions along the Powell route. If you're inexperienced with these activities, consider beginning your Powell route adventures with a guided company or a private-trip equipment outfitter and shuttle service. You'll find choices included in the chapters, along with basic info for planning your own logistics as needed.

Permits and lotteries. Another major challenge of navigating the Powell route is understanding the permit and/or lottery systems required for many of the classic trips. For more details, see the relevant segments and sections in the chapters. The hardest permit to obtain is for private trips in the Grand Canyon, which requires submitting a lottery application to Grand Canyon National Park in February, roughly 1 year in advance. The second hardest permit to obtain is for a Lodore trip in Dinosaur National Monument; it should be submitted by the end of January for trips during the high season of the same year. A Desolation Trip, managed by the BLM, is the third-hardest permit to obtain via lottery application and should be submitted by the end of January. Labyrinth Canyon involves a self-issue permit from the BLM. Stillwater and Cataract trips require a permit request made to Canyonlands National Park no less than 2 days prior to launch. Glen Canyon backhaul and Black Canyon of the Colorado require advance reservations with private outfitters for access to the launch locations. You're turning blue! Why are you turning blue? Breathe. Breathe, dammit!

Camping. There's tremendous variety to the camping situations found along the route, so find specific info and regulations in each chapter. Generally, there are few reserved or assigned sites outside Red Canyon and Dino. There are a few float-in campgrounds on reservoirs and some riverside campgrounds here and there. In other places, commercial and private groups have established unofficial sites over the years, while in the Grand Canyon, the suitable sites have long been found and named by boaters but remain first come, first camped. When crossing wakes with other groups, it's common to exchange pleasantries and agreeable camping plans. In general, spring high-water makes camping trickier, as many sandbar sites are flooded, though sometimes higher terraces can be reached to compensate. Carrying tents or rain shelters is advisable at all times, but during warm seasons, many paddlers sleep on sandy beaches, which become increasingly available as water levels drop. Mosquito shelters are advisable for certain times and places. ***Caution:*** Avoid camping in dry washes. These are ephemeral creeks that can flash in a hurry, full of raging debris flows that may come from distant storms and may be unseen or unheard. Curious? Search online for videos about flash floods in canyon camps.

Stars. You should expect a lot of these . . .

EQUIPMENT FOR THE ROUTE

We paddlers live in an era when adventure sports are so popular we have countless options for outdoor equipment, technical outerwear, and exploration accessories. This isn't 1869, when "cutting edge" meant wooden Whitehall rowboats, spare oars made from driftwood, and tree sap for adhesive. Now we have thermoformed plastic kayaks, carbon fiber oars, and Aquaseal. Yay, us?

Well, mostly. Along with logistics, assembling the equipment needed for desert river trips is one of the biggest challenges along the Powell route. A good rule of thumb is to recognize that some items are necessities for certain trips while other items are luxuries—nice to have but not required. The discussion that follows is here to help sort through the onslaught of adventure gear so you don't use those thumbs to gouge your eyes out.

Boats. You'll need one of these, but there's no single boat that's perfect for the entire Powell route. Luckily, there are rental options along much of the route. Inflatable rafts are the most popular choice for the whitewater sections and many of the flatwater multidays. Most rafts are *oar rigs*, aka *gear rafts*, rowed by a single (and often looking) rower and loaded down with an obscene collection of gear. We're talking camping equipment, coolers, kitchen set-up, kitchen sink, food, water, portable toilet, regular-sized toilet, two-person vanity toilet from 1980s *SNL* skit (look it up!).

A flotilla of oar rafts, duckies (inflatable kayaks), and "lazy" play-boaters (who examine every rapid first, like it's fine wine, before committing to anything) motor through upper Desolation Canyon.

Most rafts are 14 to 18 feet, but smaller and even—wait for it—larger sizes are possible. Catarafts and paddlecats are similar but have two pontoon tubes joined by an inner frame or compartment. Guided paddle rafts are less common along the route mostly due to flatwater and distances, but they're a fun and active alternative for day trips or instead of riding in a gear raft. Motor rigs can be regular rafts with a transom and motor, often stowed during whitewater, or custom jobs that extend 20 to 30 feet and plow through rapids like dirt-bags commandeering an aquatic bus. Whitewater dories and fishing drift boats are hard-hulled modern rowboats that look like a huge blast, but no one's ever invited me (single teardrop).

Kayaks are the second most popular choice and often accompany raft-supported trips, especially in the Grand Canyon but also in other sections, especially those with whitewater. Inflatable kayaks, aka duckies or IKs, are popular during warm-weather trips and are easy to paddle—they can also be loaded with gear for multidays. Self-support kayak trips typically involve touring or sea kayaks for flatwater sections (though advanced paddlers will take them through everything) or whitewater-touring hybrids and long boats. Stand-up paddleboards (SUPs) are increasingly popular along the route, particularly in flatwater sections or on raft trips—though whitewater and self-support use is growing. Packrafts are ultra-light IKs that can be carried on foot and combined with canyoneering and hiking trips. Canoes are great for flatwater river sections and reservoirs, depending on comfort with wind and waves. Phew . . . what else? In 1867, James White infamously claimed to have floated the entire Grand Canyon on logs. While it probably never happened, that does sound like fun. But today it's illegal. They'll take your logs away.

Safety and specialty equipment. One way to decide which items are necessary is by asking: Do I need this for safety reasons? Does it protect against hazards typically encountered along the route? On the highly regulated portions, managing agencies mandate certain equipment based upon common situations, and their checklists (discussed below) provide a basic outline of required equipment. Elsewhere, you'll have to decide for yourself.

Some items, like a properly fitting PFD (lifejacket) with adequate flotation, are obvious. These keep your head above water during accidental swims through aerated water and swift rapids. But often forgotten is the hazard of hypothermia from cold-water immersion, which is still possible in a hot desert during summer. With varying potential for upsets during flatwater and whitewater, a paddler must consider how much insulation is needed. A splash jacket (like a raincoat with tighter cuffs) and wetsuit are the cheapest option, while advanced but expensive dry tops and dry suits are more comfortable and are often worn by avid paddlers for harder whitewater and colder water and seasons.

Regarding helmets, whitewater kayakers always wear them due to the hazard of flipping over amid rocks. Rafters tend to carry them to wear during harder rapids or high water, often to avoid impacts with their own raft should it flip. A throw rope or wrap kit is important and often required. But you must use these properly, meaning take a swift-water rescue training course. Without knowledge and instruction, hurling a loose rope at a panicking and flailing swimmer can make a situation worse by dangerously entangling them.

Another hazard is shifting weather and changing temperatures. Even on flatwater day-trips, air temps may drop suddenly, meaning an accessible bag of synthetic or wool layers becomes a safety item. Using watertight dry bags (folding or zipped) becomes necessary for keeping sleeping bags and camp clothing dry to combat cold nights. A tent that can withstand rain and wind is important—you don't need the best and most expensive model, but a cheaper, low-quality tent may fall apart. Similarly, a decent raincoat is strongly recommended.

Because of remoteness and limited access, resupply is typically impossible or difficult. That means food must be protected by proper packaging, coolers, dry bags, or dry boxes to avoid water damage and spoiling. Dehydration is another concern; emergency treatment tablets, a hand pump or electric filter, and extra water containers become necessary. Protection from sun exposure requires combinations of hats, sleeves, lotions, umbrellas, and sunglasses. Plus, while loading and unloading all this stuff, keep in mind that rugged shorelines and camps have sharp rocks and thorny plants, so good footwear is necessary. Even old tennis shoes can work—yes, they're gonna smell terrible once wet, but most of the other stuff will smell terrible, too.

When you add together all the needed equipment, it's easy to see why rafts have become the default boat along the route. Self-support kayaking is an amazing experience, but it requires experience with more advanced and packable equipment that can fit inside smaller boats.

Required equipment. Along the Powell route, certain items—typically for purposes of safety, sanitization, and conservation—are required by the managing agencies on various parts of the route. Such agencies provide detailed checklists to permit recipients, which can be found in the relevant chapters. Although such items are not required by an agency on other parts of the route, experienced paddlers independently choose to carry many of these items for the same reasons. They include adequate first-aid kits, repair kits, pumps for inflatables, helmets, and spray skirts for kayaks, and relevant spares—including oars, paddles, and PFDs. Sanitization, cleaning, and trash procedures often involve biodegradable soap, hand sanitizer, washing buckets, and trash bags that are stowed in watertight containers. Some agencies require charcoal or wood fires be contained within metal firepans, which can often double as grilling surfaces. In some sections, all fire ash and coals must be carried out as trash. There's more to it than I can list here, but one final item to repeat: All human solid waste must be removed from many segments and sections along the Powell route. The reason is that the campsites are in high-use desert areas, where even natural wastes will quickly accumulate and can't break down in a timely manner. To remove this requires renting or owning an approved toilet system, which is carried down the river. And, yes, this has led to some interesting . . . situations. For a few of the best (worst), check out the hilarious book: *Up Shit Creek: A Collection of Horrifyingly True Wilderness Toilet Misadventures* by rafter Joe Lindsay.

Camping and cooking equipment. Some large groups of lifelong rafters will unload what appears to be a full kitchen they stole from a gourmet restaurant at every camp on a 21-day Grand Canyon trip. These camp-life connoisseurs bring a half dozen folding and rolling tables, six-burner stoves, and enough pots and pans to cater a civil war

For many Powell route paddlers, camp life is an important part of the experience.

siege with steak and lobster. Groups with moderate meal ambitions—perhaps smaller raft and canoe trips focused on hiking and exploring—might sneak by with a two-burner stove, cooking basic meals with some fresh food supplemented by canned food and pasta on a single breakdown table. Other groups, often kayakers, move fast and light with ultralight backpacking stoves and dehydrated meals. Whatever your preference, it can be helpful to develop your approach through two methods: First, observe experienced groups— say, on a commercial trip or with experienced friends. Second, consider adapting cooking methods developed in other self-contained outdoor activities. RV camping is great preparation for river-camp connoisseurs. Car camping road trips are great preparation for moderately ambitious rafting chefs. And backpacking shares many characteristics with self-support kayaking.

Caution: Because of the tendency for gear to shift during paddling, always protect your "sharps." This is especially true for inflatable rafts. Use folding knives or those with latching sheathes. Same for hatchets or saws. Many groups avoid glass jars and bottles, transferring everything to plastic or aluminum containers. Other groups will cover a few glass items in duct tape so that if they break, they don't spread shards in boxes, bags, and boats.

> "THE FLOUR HAS BEEN RESIFTED THROUGH THE MOSQUITO-NET SIEVE; THE SPOILED BACON HAS BEEN DRIED AND THE WORST OF IT BOILED; THE FEW POUNDS OF DRIED APPLES HAVE BEEN SPREAD IN THE SUN AND RESHRUNKEN TO THEIR NORMAL BULK. THE SUGAR HAS ALL MELTED AND GONE ON ITS WAY DOWN RIVER. BUT WE HAVE A LARGE SACK OF COFFEE."
> —*John Wesley Powell*

Luxury equipment. Not counting life-saving medicines, it's pretty common to hear luxury items for a paddling trip described this way: "I couldn't live without my [blanks]." I've seen some interesting "blanks" pop up in the outdoors, and mostly in good fun. One time, while guiding a backpacking trip high in the Sierra Nevadas, I watched a guest pull from her pack a CD player, stereo speakers, a half-dozen albums, and a giant bag of batteries—putting the whole set-up around 10 pounds. *"I couldn't live without my music!"*

But who am I to talk? My buddy and I once carried a whole wet bar over a mountain to an alpine lake for a weekend reunion. Add in the extra dry-bag space of a river trip, and not even a dark sky is the limit. How about disco balls and strobes illuminating river canyon dance parties? Christmas lights strung across campsites. All powered by portable solar panels and rechargeable batteries.

In the analog world, whole libraries might be stacked on tree stumps. Rain shelters are also there to house board games, felt poker tables, even river sauna tents. Some groups transport a costume closet, which would rival a wedding photo booth, for tacky Tuesdays in Granite Gorge. Plus, horseshoes, bocci ball, Frisbee golf—it's not *if* but *when* the first four-team volleyball tournament will be held in Redwall Cavern.

Even just coolers, which most raft groups would say are absolutely required, are (very welcome) luxuries. Having fresh foods, fresh meats, fresh veggies, fresh fruits makes a long river trip that much more enjoyable. And that brings us to one final item:

Ice-cold beer in camp? Hey, I'm gonna say river trip necessity, but please discuss among yourselves.

RESOURCES: BOOKS, FILMS, MUSEUMS, AND COURSES

Powell route boaters often enhance their experiences with supplementary readings from the original expeditions, later explorers, historians, scientists, and more. Some pilgrims collect every book and guide on the subject, dragging a partial library down the river in nearly sinking boats. (Guilty.) I've read more than fifty relevant books, and I wish I could list them all. Instead, here I've focused on those most relevant to curious novices—plus, I mention more books and guides in the segments. The more you learn about the route, the more interesting your trips may become.

Books. *The Exploration of the Colorado River and Its Canyons* by John Wesley Powell, 1875. The most popular account should certainly be read, but it may not be the best to start with. For various reasons, Powell combined experiences from the 1871–72 expedition into his account of the first, in 1869, as if it were all one gloriously successful trip. Umm . . . His book is full of inaccuracies and exaggerations in addition to some outstanding passages that certainly deserve to be preserved for posterity. Powell was more of a politician than a river runner, and his account is more semifictional dramatization than factual nonfiction. It also starts with more than one hundred pages of exposition that's probably best appreciated by those familiar with the region or those with a topography fetish, which is a real thing. Powell did many great things—from conceiving and organizing the expeditions, to cataloging the geology and topography, to visiting with Native American tribes and recording their languages and mythologies throughout the West—but the dude could have used an editor.

Down the Great Unknown by Edward Dolnick, 2001. This narrative nonfiction account dramatizes the first expedition and makes an entertaining primer for the novice pilgrim. Dolnick tells the tale with a great deal of energy. An enjoyable way to enter a long conversation about the first expedition.

A Canyon Voyage: The Narrative of the Second Powell Expedition by Frederick S. Dellenbaugh, 1926. This engaging account of the second expedition, by a crew member and artist, is well written and entertaining. Only 17 years old at the time, he conveys the experience with genuine enthusiasm and remarkable attention to detail. Some critics have noted that he clearly considered Powell a lifelong hero and mentor. And Dellenbaugh also sided with Powell by excluding the three men who left the first

Paddling the Powell route? Bring a bookshelf!

expedition, and vanished, from a commemorative plaque on the South Rim, further-ing the narrative that the men were cowardly deserters. Regardless, this is a remarkable adventure tale that offers a nice view on both expeditions. Dellenbaugh's *Romance of the Colorado* is also a worthy read.

Beyond the Hundredth Meridian: John Wesley Powell and the Second Opening of the West by Wallace Stegner, 1953. A broad look at Powell's career and accomplishments before, during, and after the expeditions. Placing Powell's life in a broader context of the time period, this is a great book for a wide view on Powell. Plus, it's EFFing Wallace Stegner.

First through Grand Canyon: The Secret Journals and Letters of the 1869 Crew Who Explored the Green and Colorado Rivers by Michael P. Ghiglieri, 2003. River guide and historian Ghiglieri created one of greatest books imaginable for Powell pilgrims by not only collecting all known primary source materials created by members of the 1869 expedition in one volume, but also by correcting errors carried down from original transcriptions. There's also fascinating research by Ghiglieri and historian Don Lago, who recently offered his own interesting revisionist history volume, *Powell Expedition*, 2017. While Ghiglieri's criticism of Powell seems overreaching at times, almost per-sonal, his is one of the best revisionist histories about the first expedition and is worth a close read.

Colorado River Controversies by Robert Brewster Stanton, 1932. Published posthu-mously more than a decade after it was written, this book is the first to examine key inconsistencies about Powell's account of the expedition, plus an examination of James White's claim of descending the Grand Canyon first on a log raft. An exacting engineer, Stanton was involved in a few disastrous expeditions down the Grand Can-yon and was determined to build a railroad through its depths.

There are dozens of other worthy books for Powell route pilgrims, from the *Diary of Almon Harris Thompson*, who, during land-based exploration on the second expedi-tion, mapped the Escalante River, the final major river named by whites in the United States. A pair of beautifully written books by naturalist Anne Zwinger, *Run, River, Run* (1975) about the Green River, and *Down Canyon* (1995) about the Colorado River. *The Emerald Mile* by Kevin Fedarko (2013), an entertaining story about the fastest descent of the Grand Canyon by dory during the floods of 1983. *A River Running West* by Donald Worster presents Powell as an environmental hero far ahead of his time. And *From Powell to Power*, written by Dock Marsten and edited by Tom Martin,

Find more great books and films in the online shop of the Grand Canyon Association at grandcanyon.org, plus gift shops and websites of museums and visitor centers.

which meticulously recounts the first one hundred river runners through the Grand Canyon. The book can be tedious at times, but the real value is the humorous subtext of Marsten's commentary, which has all the charms of a riverside heckler gossiping about passing groups.

Films. Surprisingly, there's not a lot about the expeditions. A "favorite" film for river runners to make fun of (despite few ever watching) is Disney's *Ten Who Dared*, 1960. JWP even got a writing credit and now has an IMDb profile, no joke. Think more midnight movie than accurate biopic (see below). *National Geographic's Grand Canyon: The Hidden Secrets* is an excellent 34-minute IMAX movie, which plays at the South Rim Visitor Center and includes a quasi-reenactment of the 1869 expedition but with more river running and less portaging than really happened, using boats resembling those used in 1871–72.

Museums. The John Wesley Powell River History Museum, in Green River, UT, is the most relevant museum, with exhibits relating to Powell, the expeditions, and later river running along the route. A real highlight is a boat room with a replica of the *No Name*, the boat wrecked in Disaster Falls of the Canyon of Lodore during 1869. There's a river runner's hall of fame, which documents famous boaters from along the route, plus other temporary exhibitions. Visit johnwesleypowell.com.

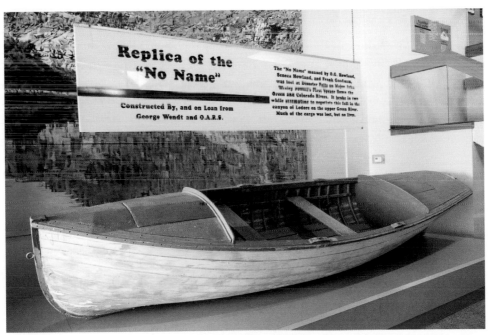

A replica of the *No Name*, destroyed at Disaster Falls in the Canyon of Lodore on the 1869 expedition, found at the JW Powell River History Museum in Green River, UT.

An old oar rests against a wall at the John Jarvie Historic Ranch in Browns Park. (Sheep shears optional on modern Powell route.)

The Powell Museum and Page Lake Powell Visitor Center, in Page, AZ, have exhibits about Powell's five trips and expeditions to the West, maps from the time period, a series of Rudolph Wendelin paintings (creator of the 1969 postage stamp), and more. Outside, you'll find a giant rowboat that was used in Disney's *Ten Who Dared*. Visit www.powellmuseum.org.

Sweetwater County Historical Museum, in Green River, WY, is focused on regional history, which offers some nice context about the area before and after the expeditions. Plus, there are several exhibits relevant to the expeditions and river exploration. Most important, there's a giant JWP statue outside—Powell selfie, anyone? Visit www .sweetwatermuseum.org.

In Green River Valley, just north of the route, there are two great museums worth checking out. At the seasonal Museum of the Mountain Man in Pinedale, WY, visitors gain insight into Native American and American activities in the region prior to the Powell expeditions, typically called the North American fur trade or mountain man era, when young men were employed by trapping companies across the region to collect beaver pelts for sale, plus a replica buffalo-hide teepee and examples of Native American and trapper dress (museumofthemountainman.com). The Green

River Valley Museum can be found in Big Piney, WY, with a focus on pioneer life in the valley during the period of white settlement that began shortly after the Powell expeditions, including artifacts and covered wagons like those that passed through the area on the Oregon Trail (www.grvm.com).

In Vernal, UT, there is the Utah Field House of Natural History, with an emphasis on dinosaur fossils and paleontology. Nearby, Dinosaur National Monument has the remarkable Quarry Exhibit Hall, where you can see actual fossilized dino bones in situ on a partially uncovered cliff face. And, of course, the Grand Canyon has several excellent museums at the south and north rims. A visit to the rim can cause even greater excitement when preceding a river trip through the canyon, while visiting the rim after a river trip might elicit a more comprehensible experience for some.

Courses and lessons. One of the biggest challenges for curious outsiders—those who don't grow up in a paddling community but become interested from afar—is how the heck to begin?! I grew up in an urban area, where the word *paddling* was more associated with corporal punishment or BDSM, depending on your age and familiarity with the internet. I became aware of the sport incrementally through trips with the Boy Scouts. Then one day it all catalyzed below Lava Rapid, on a backpacking trip to the bottom of the Grand Canyon. Soon after, I became a raft guide through a whitewater guide school, one of many courses offering an "in."

For those who may wish to divert their life in an unexpected and exhilarating direction toward the rivers of the Southwest, there are several opportunities. NOLS, the National Outdoor Leadership School, offers an amazing 16-day course for all ages, which includes learning to kayak, raft guide, and row down 125 miles of the Powell route through Deso, Lodore, and more (www.nols.edu). Colorado Outward Bound offers similar courses along the route, including Deso, Lab, and Cataract (www.cobs .org). Meanwhile, many rafting companies along the route offer whitewater guide schools and various paddling clubs or shops offer lessons and clinics.

SHUCKS, I DARE YOU TO WATCH DISNEY'S *TEN WHO DARED*

If you ever find yourself sitting on the couch in winter, waiting for spring flows to once again gush through the canyon country of the Powell expeditions, flipping through movie streaming options, and lamenting the lack of penetrating biopics about the exploits of John Wesley—this *does* sound like you, doesn't it?—well, to you I say, lament not! Walt Disney himself, in 1960, gave us Powell pilgrims our very own motion picture incarnation of a sacred text.

Sure, it's way more midnight movie—let's say, *Plan 9 from Inner Gorge* or *The Room . . . of Doom*—than it is celebrated epic like Heston's felt-like-two-dozen

A catamaran under motor power tows a spoiled canoe through Red Canyon. Get your shit together, canoe.

Commandments. And, yes, *Ten Who Dared* is pretty lacking in historical authenticity, geographic accuracy, realistic characterizations, believable boating sequences (Watch out! Someone offscreen is tossing water from buckets again!), or just plain viewability. (The years were not kind to the negatives.)

But the film more than makes up for all the missteps with goofy Disney fun. Post-war mood disorders that come and go with a snap of the fingers? Check. A boatmen song-and-dance routine that would make a modern Grand Canyon sandbar party jealous? Check. A heavy-handed philosophical struggle between scientific observation and astrology almanacs? Plenty of wet man-on-man fistfights with a splash of hero worship? A shootout with a whisky keg? An odd product placement for hominy? Some light stalking? Gold-panning subplot? Staring contest with a rattlesnake? Yes, yes, yes!

Did I mention *Ten Who Dared* has a dog? A smuggled puppy with more plot-significant barks than some characters have lines. Fun fact: The dog's name may be a reference to the John Jarvie Historic Ranch in Browns Park, which was established in 1880 and can be still be visited. In general, the screenwriters clearly did plenty of research into the Powell expeditions, even if they chose to drastically adapt what they found. A Native American legend buried in the final chapters of Powell's 1875 book makes a dramatized appearance. The tensions between the three who left and the Powell brothers are there. And the fate of those three, who disappeared and were presumed murdered, is left somewhat ambiguous, suggesting that even in 1960 there were those questioning the validity of the long-accepted mythology.

I'm just waiting for someone to haul a projector and screen down to Trin Alcove Bend for an on-river matinee. Never in cinematic history has baking biscuits, fossil hunting, and desert hiking been more dramatic than in *Ten Who Dared*. Okay, maybe *Indiana Jones*.

How to Use This Book

Read this book, put it down, go paddle? Okay, I'm being told to try that again. You can use this book to plan amazing river trips! As a gift for avid paddlers, curious beginners, veteran pilgrims, and armchair adventurers! To look at pretty pictures! I guess as a beverage coaster? To keep other books in your bookshelf from not falling down? Okay, I'm being yelled at. (Nothing new.)

Putting this book together was a challenge, as it covers 1,600 miles of river across six states—the "official" 1,000-mile Powell route, plus 200 miles above and 400 below. The goal was a broad inspirational guide that helps readers identify and plan trips along that extended thematic route. To achieve this goal, we had to make some tough decisions about what to include or leave out. Instead of topographic maps, which would have taken at least 100 pages, we opted for plenty of color photos to help paddlers visualize the sections. But the result is that paddlers must acquire supplementary topo maps or guides for navigation—with options listed in the segments. Meanwhile,

Perched on the rim above Flaming Gorge Reservoir, about 75 paddling miles from Green River, WY, the Red Canyon visitor center is a perfect spot to contemplate *Why am I not paddling that?*

the basic maps included are designed to help locate the sections, segments, and some points of interest with reference to location along the route.

In addition to describing a wide variety of trips—from a few hours' duration to a few weeks—I've also mentioned some hikes, petroglyphs, ruins, waterfalls, and compelling rocks (not apologizing). But there are too many to list! Thus, I also point out other books, guides, and readings. Plus, keep your eyes and ears open out there. The more you put into the Powell route, the more you'll enrich your experiences on the water.

Organizationally, this book is divided into eleven chapters, each providing a longer river segment along the route. The segments are further divided into shorter sections that range from day trips to multidays. Because of access and permitting situations, some segments have just one section, while others have a half dozen. Sometimes, certain short sections overlap other longer sections within the same section. (Coffee break!)

Every segment lists details essential for planning trips. When those details apply to the entire segment, they appear under "Segment Details." When those details are only relevant to a specific section, they go into "Section Details." A few details that span multiple segments are relocated to sidebars. (Phew. Can you make me a cup, too?) If this seems complicated, then—*ding, ding, ding*   that's because the Powell route *is* complicated. But so very much worth the effort.

This book assumes that a paddler might want to paddle reservoirs in the same direction, generally north to south, as the expeditions once followed the preflooded rivers. However, one could travel the three reservoirs in the reverse direction. In fact, doing so might even be easier, as the prevailing winds tend to move mostly up-canyon from the south or southwest. That said, if you're set on being a Powell route pilgrim, why do anything the easy way when you can do it the *right* way and block the silly wind with sunglasses.

LET LARS HAARR FROM OARS BE YOUR GUIDE ON THE POWELL ROUTE

Named best river guide of 2015 by *Outside* magazine, Lars Haarr has guided since 1999 for OARS, a commercial outfitter running every permitted section along the Powell route. A lifelong river rat, Lars grew up in Montana, and he's since boated rivers in South America, British Columbia, and across the United States—including countless guided trips along the Powel route. Here he shares valuable advice for those deciding to go it alone or join a guided trip.

Campfire on an OARS trip in Cataract Canyon. For more awesome adventure photography, visit www.whitrichardson.com! WHIT RICHARDSON.

Mike: For folks who are new to the Powell route, how do you suggest they start?

Lars: First, decide if you're a do-it-yourself person or pay-your-way guest. For DIYers, definitely start with the logistically easier stretches, like Red Canyon in a ducky or Labyrinth in a canoe.

Our guests join a commercial trip for many different reasons. Perhaps they lack the skills and equipment to set out on their own. Maybe they've done some camping or canoeing but no whitewater rafting. Maybe they were adventurous earlier in their lives but have slowed down and are looking for catered, comfy camping. Or maybe they value having a guide along to share intimate knowledge of the place. On our trips, guests pitch in as little or as much as they want—there's certainly a sense of satisfaction when someone who's never camped before properly sets up a tent on the first try! A lot of camaraderie happens when the "tribe" comes together.

Another option is a combination of do-it-yourself and pay-to-play trips. Obtaining permits for Lodore and the Grand Canyon is tough. The private permit is very difficult to get, and even our commercial trips are booked 2 years in advance. You could join OARS for certain stretches, with tricky lotteries or harder whitewater, and link them with DIY self-support trips.

If you have no river experience, whitewater or otherwise, learning how to boat would be a great start. OARS offers a couple different guide schools, one of which is based in Vernal. This would enable someone to at least tackle the easier stretches on their own!

Mike: Can you describe a typical day on a guided trip?

Lars: A typical day starts early, with coffee and breakfast prepared by the guides. Soon after breakfast, guides load the boats while guests pack up personal stuff. After "Last call on the toilet!" we head downstream. There might be a hike before lunch, or maybe some calm water floating, or perhaps some rapids. Then lunch, typically on a riverside beach. After lunch, more of the same until a suitable campsite is reached. While dinner is being made, guests enjoy cold beverages while laughing and sharing the day's events. Some nights feature a campfire, and many a tall tale has been woven after dinner to the sound of a crackling fire. Eventually, the stories wane, pillows call, and we sleep with a million stars shining brightly overhead. Next day, rinse and repeat!

Mike: Okay, I'm in! So does Powell come up at all?

Lars: No matter the stretch, JWP plays an important part. We talk about the expedition and its effects on modern-day river running. Nightly discussions often include readings from his journal, debates on portaging versus lining rapids, or how on earth a man with one arm did it! He is held in the highest regard, despite his gruff military style of leadership. One of the stories we often tell is when Powell and Bradley climb for the rim and JWP gets cliffed-out and writes, "The moment is critical. My muscles tremble. It occurs to Bradley to take off his drawers." Comical, yet what a terrifying adventure! I feel more of a connection, knowing that perhaps these brave men once stood exactly where I regularly place my feet.

Mike: What are some of your favorite places and river sections along the route?

Lars: Each section of river has its own voice and mood, depending on time of year. It would be impossible for me to choose. It's like asking a parent which kid is their favorite! The Cataract trip is one I've done the most—probably 250-plus times—and my favorite rapid is Big Drop 2, especially at high water. But, I feel the other, lesser-known stretches are amazing, too. Some of my absolute favorites are Stars with Lars trips. The first is in April on the San Juan, followed by a second in September on Cataract. We discuss cosmology, learn about constellations, and, of course, look at the stars. I bring a small telescope along, and we check out any visible planets or other deep-space objects. The canyons are very deep with sheer walls. While this limits how much sky you can see, these canyons are typically some of the darkest places around. In fact, some of the Powell route passes through official International Dark Sky–certi-fied parks. All you have to do is look up!

Driving Directions Disclaimer

The GPS coordinates provided for access locations in the segment chapters are for planning and reference purposes only and not recommended for use with GPS navigation programs for many access points. Relying blindly upon GPS navigation along the Powell route can lead river runners onto un-maintained, abandoned, or dangerous roads. During my trips to the desert and along the Powell route, I have more than once aided lost travelers, sometimes with disabled vehicles, who insisted on following incorrect directions from a navigation program. I have drawn crude maps to the nearest gas station, supplied drinking water, and helped push vehicles stuck in sand. Been helped myself a few times. The roads that I list in the logistics sections are the suggested routes commonly used by experienced paddlers and shuttle companies. There are often other (and possibly rougher) routes that some drivers use, depending on their comfort level and vehicle capabilities. I strongly recommend that first-time Powell route paddlers conduct supplementary research into current road conditions. Carry paper maps and stay aware. It's a desert out there.

Trip Finder by Duration and Character

Use these lists to find trips of the duration and character you're looking for. They might also work for bragging rights at a riverside name-dropping party. From left to right, you'll find segment number, abbreviated section name, and a brief description.

DAY TRIPS ALONG THE POWELL ROUTE

0 Green River Lakes. *A pair of scenic lakes beneath the Wind River Range.*

0 Seedskadee National Wildlife Refuge. *A relaxing class I float below Fontenelle Dam.*

1 Flaming Gorge Reservoir. *Open desert and scenic canyons.*

2 Red Canyon. *Sections A and B have great scenery, class II rapids, clear waters.*

2 Browns Park. *Fall off the map with a class I float through a wild western valley.*

3 Split Mountain daily. *Rainbow Park to Split in Dino, NM, with class II–III rapids.**

4 Split to Jensen. *Class I float from geologic drama to foothills of Uinta Basin.*

4 Ouray National Wildlife Refuge. *Lazy class I river through remote wildlife refuge.*

5 Green River daily. *Sporty class II rapids through the end of Gray Canyon.*

8 Lake Powell. *Many reservoir day trips, including Antelope Canyon, etc.*

8 Glen Canyon backhaul. *Remnants of Glen Canyon offer class I float and lofty heights.*

10 Lake Mead. *A remote, empty landscape near Temple Bay.*

10 Lower Colorado River. *Winter options on rivers and reservoirs.*

2- TO 4-DAY TRIPS ALONG THE POWELL ROUTE

0 Green River Lakes. *Paddle through a scenic delta to camp on an alpine lake.*

1 Flaming Gorge Reservoir. *Start where Powell did or visit the first canyons.*

2 Red Canyon. *Combine A and B sections for classic overnight.*

NOLS kayaking students Brian Finci and Ben Baltimore having a blast on Moonshine Rapids in Split Mountain Canyon of the Green River. KIRK RASMUSSEN/NOLS

2 Browns Park. *Add C section to above, plus a wildlife refuge, or paddle separately.*

3 Lodore to Split. *Twisty geology + class III rapids = best 4-day trip on Powell route.***

4 Uinta Basin. *Several options for short class I multiday trips.*

6 Labyrinth Canyon. *A great flatwater 4-day winds through startling sandstones.**

8 Lake Powell. *Several out-n-backs or through-paddling options.*

8 Glen Canyon backhaul. *Most paddlers do this 15-mile stretch in 2 days.*

9 Diamond Down. *The bottom portion of Grand Canyon in a long weekend.**

10 Black Canyon of the Colorado. *Hot spring overload on the "Vegas of float streams."**

5- TO 10-DAY TRIPS ALONG THE POWELL ROUTE

1 Flaming Gorge Reservoir. *A week-long trip from expedition start through first canyons.*

2 Red Canyon to Gates. *Drop off the map over 5 days, class II–I.*

4 Uinta Basin. *Through-paddle a forgotten river of low bluffs and lazy river, class I.*

5 Deso/Gray. *This week-long trip is a class II amusement park for paddlers.***

6 Lab and Stillwater. *100+ miles of flatwater through Canyonlands National Park.**

7 Cataract Canyon. *Some of the best whitewater, class III–IV, along the route.**

8 Lake Powell. *Through-paddle this controversial and scenic reservoir.*

10+ DAY TRIPS ALONG THE POWELL ROUTE

Many of the above sections and segments can be combined in various ways, but let's not delay:

9 Grand Canyon. *It's the best, how could it not be? (class III-IV)***

* These trips involve obtaining a permit, which may or may not be limited, but do not involve a lottery.

** These trips involve obtaining a permit that requires winning a lottery application, either for launches year-round or for those during high season.

Map Legend

≡(15)≡	Interstate	▭	National Park/Monument
≡(40)≡	U.S. Highway	▣	National Recreation Area/Refuge
≡(313)≡	State Road	▲	Peak
⊏222⊐	Local/County Road	■	Point of Interest/Trailhead
- - - - - - -	Trail	*1*	Powell Route Mileage Marker
- - — - - -	International Border	⌐¬	Reservation
- - - — -	State Border	◪	Scenic View
⬭	Body of Water	○	Town
～	River/Creek	?	Visitor Center
▲	Access	≋	Waterfall
⏶	Campground		

UPPER GREEN RIVER AND LAKES

UPSTREAM FROM THE ACTUAL START OF THE POWELL ROUTE, there is over 200 miles of valley river and mountain lakes often forgotten by paddlers infatuated with the famous desert sections below. But in southwestern Wyoming, there is much of relevance to the Powell route and plenty of highlights worth visiting for their own merits.

The Green River begins its 730-mile course—toward a confluence with the Colorado River in Canyonlands National Park—as an alpine stream emerging from glaciers just west of the continental divide in the Wind River Range. While the uppermost

While exploring lower Green River Lake, I hung out with two families of lifelong boaters, including a pair of exceptionally bright teenage daughters and a baby boy given the middle name "Powell," for family hero John Wesley.

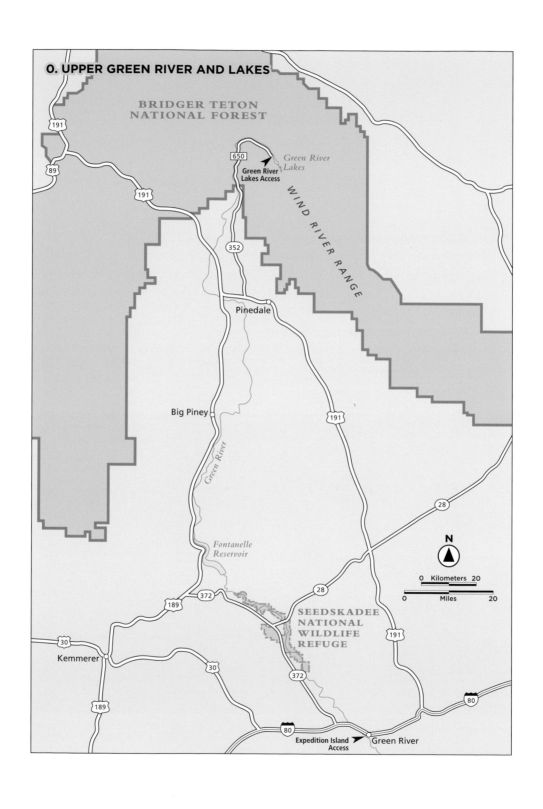

O. UPPER GREEN RIVER AND LAKES

BRIDGER TETON
NATIONAL FOREST

650

Green River
Lakes

Green River
Lakes Access

WIND RIVER RANGE

191

89

191

352

Pinedale

Big Piney

Green River

191

28

Fontanelle
Reservoir

N

0   Kilometers   20

0   Miles   20

372

189

28

SEEDSKADEE
NATIONAL
WILDLIFE
REFUGE

191

30

Kemmerer

30

372

189

80

80

Expedition Island
Access

Green River

The October basecamp used by Zak and Will to explore the headwaters of the Green River in the Wind River Range. WILL STAUFFER-NORRIS

headwaters, within Teton-Bridger National Forest, are best explored on foot, plenty of scenic paddling can be found at Green River Lakes and nearby stretches of the river.

The upper Green River has a curious trajectory, first aiming northwest as it emerges from the glacial-carved Winds, before making a sharp, sweeping bend south, as if saying, "Screw this, I'm going somewhere warmer." Downstream from the lakes, the Green flows through peaceful meadows and tumbles down occasional class II rapids, bordering on class III at higher spring flows, before slackening into braids and meandering through Green River Valley.

Though this chapter focuses on just two sections of the upper Green—the lakes and Seedskadee Wildlife Refuge—plenty more is worth exploring, and paddlers could spend

The Floater's Guide to Wyoming by Dan Lewis covers the 200 miles of the upper Green River. Published in 1991 and now out of print, the guide is available in its entirety on the author's website: wyomingnaturalist.com.

Quiet stretches of the upper Green River offer ample float and fish opportunities, whether by drift boat, kayak, paddleboard . . .

more than a week in this area. In addition to paddling, the hiking near the lakes is some of the most dramatic found outside of national parks. And two valley museums (see page xlii) give insight into Western life in the periods before and after the Powell expeditions.

PADDLING: GREEN RIVER LAKES

If you paddle only one of the five lakes and reservoirs featured in this guide—for the sake of dramatic scenery and remarkable variety compared to canyon country—consider lower Green River Lake. If you paddle only two lakes, then why not send a subtle dig to the Bureau of Reclamation by paddling up through a pristine delta and camping beside the milky turquoise waters of upper Green River Lake? From there, motivated paddlers can navigate a few more miles of upper river toward Squaretop Mountain before beaching boats and exploring on foot. A hiking and horse trail follows the river to its headwaters at the Great Divide and continues beyond, offering excellent but challenging backpacking options. The fishing on the lakes and surrounding river is considered top-notch by visiting anglers. And downstream from the lakes, there are plenty of paddling opportunities, which can be scouted and accessed from the gravel road.

Duration: One minute to all of eternity; paddling to the upper lake and beyond is at least a half day and probably a full day with side explorations and hiking.

Access: Gravel boat ramp at Green River Lakes Recreation Area (N43 18.65' / W109 51.44').

Paddling upstream on the upper Green River above the upper lake. Do you see a theme to this caption?

The Continental Divide Trail follows the lakes and upper Green River beneath Squaretop Mountain.

"THE GENERAL COURSE OF THE RIVER IS FROM NORTH TO SOUTH AND FROM GREAT ALTITUDES TO THE LEVEL OF THE SEA. THUS IT RUNS *FROM LAND OF SNOW TO LAND OF SUN.*"

—John Wesley Powell

Logistics: Starting from the northern terminus of WY 352, at the USFS boundary, Green River Lakes Road is 19 miles of gravel that parallels the Green River. The road is well maintained but can get a bit choppy in places. Two-wheel drive (2WD) vehicles with normal clearance will be slow but fine, except during adverse weather conditions.

Season and weather: Late spring–early fall; thunderstorms and changeable weather are common; prepare for cold temps at night; snow is possible anytime; lake elevation 8,000'.

Challenges and safety: Wind can be an issue, creating waves on the lake. This is grizzly bear country, so secure food and smellables accordingly, and consider bear spray for the backcountry.

Boats: Canoe, kayak, SUP, raft, and drift boat on lake and some river sections.

Camping: Green River Lakes campground has 39 individual campsites, nonreservable, which tend to fill on summer holiday weekends but otherwise should have space. Three group sites can be reserved through www.recreation.gov. No permit required to camp in the backcountry or beside the lakes, but campers must follow leave-no-trace principles (see page xxx).

Supplies: Groceries and restaurants in Pinedale; there are a few resorts/lodges with stores near where the pavement ends.

Regulations, agencies, fees: USFS has two nearby ranger stations: 29 Fremont Lake Rd., Pinedale, WY (307) 367-4326; and 10418 US 189, Big Piney, WY (307) 276-3375; no fees other than the campground.

Maps: The USFS offers a waterproof topo map available online or at the ranger stations listed above: Bridger-Teton National Forest: Pinedale Ranger District and Bridger Wilderness. USGS 7.5 min: Green River Lakes.

PADDLING: SEEDSKADEE NATIONAL WILDLIFE REFUGE

Through a high desert prairie with riparian woodlands, low bluffs, and glimpses of the Wind River Range in the distance, the 36 miles of Green River in Seedskadee National Wildlife Refuge offer peaceful day trips on class I–II river. Just upstream, Fontenelle Dam provides a steady release of cool, clear waters popular among fishermen and warm-weather paddlers. Camping is not available within the refuge, but there are several riverside campgrounds just upstream. Most paddlers opt for upper refuge sections above WY 28, due to better roads and clearer water. Downstream river sections, especially below the confluence with the Big Sandy, are siltier, more remote, and have rougher road access. Through-paddlers will need to pass beyond in one long

Green River Valley, seen here near La Barge, offers plenty of paddling for those who go looking. WILL STAUFFER-NORRIS

day or stash a car midway to drive out of the refuge for the night. According to the US Fish & Wildlife Service, the name *Seedskadee* is derived from the Shoshone word *Sisk-a-dee-agie*, meaning "river of the prairie hen." The refuge is home to over 250 migratory and resident species, including eagles, swans, antelope, elk, and sage grouse. Wildlife sightings, especially during early mornings and early evenings, are common. Check out the refuge's Flickr page to see moose picturesquely crossing the river.

Duration: Only day trips allowed within the refuge; various lengths from 5 to over 20 miles.

Access: There are four access points inside the refuge and two upstream; see refuge website.

Logistics: Self-shuttle using either WY 372 (La Barge Rd.) or WY 28 (Lower Farson Cutoff Rd.). Most river access roads inside the refuge are gravel; north of WY 28, the gravel roads are maintained and should be fine for all vehicles during normal weather conditions. South of WY 28, the gravel roads are unimproved and rougher.

Season and weather: Spring–fall; the river banks typically ice over during winter; thunderstorms and inclement weather possible year-round; refuge elevation is approximately 6,500'.

Sometimes figuring out the Powell route can make a paddler's head spin, kinda like this dam turbine.

STATE-BY-STATE WATERCRAFT REGULATIONS

Most states along the Powell route have particular regulations concerning nonmotorized watercraft, like kayaks and rafts. A primary goal of the invasive species decal and cleaning programs is to prevent the spread of quagga and zebra mussels. These invasive mussels are both originally from Russia and Eastern Europe and can spread rapidly throughout infected waterways. A few of the problems include encrusting beaches, docks, and boat hulls; clogging engines or irrigation pipes; killing native mussels; and spreading diseases or toxins to birds and other animals. Typical cleaning procedures involve washing any boats that may have been in infected waters, then allowing the boats to dry for about a week, which kills the mussels, before using the boats in noninfected waters. **Note:** All states along the Powell route require a PFD be carried or worn at all times.

Wyoming. Depending on the time of year and the location of recent use, watercraft entering Wyoming must be inspected at an authorized location. An aquatic invasive species decal must be purchased and displayed on all watercraft using Wyoming waters, with a few nonmotorized exceptions. More info at wgfd.wyo.gov/ais.

Utah. All vehicles carrying watercraft must stop at roadside inspection stations. Boaters must conduct a self-inspection and display a self-certification form on the dashboard of their vehicle. Sometimes, the forms can be found at access locations, but not at many of the remote access points along the route. Download a single-use or annual certification form here: stdofthesea.utah.gov.

Colorado. Since the route only traverses Colorado within Dinosaur National Monument, NPS regulations apply for that segment.

Arizona requires that watercraft be cleaned and self-inspected for invasive mussels.

California: No decal is currently required for nonmotorized watercraft, but cleaning procedures are required.

Nevada. Invasive mussels were found in Lake Mead in 2007, and they've since been exposed to the Colorado River and reservoirs downstream. For nonmotorized watercraft, like kayaks and rafts, Nevada requires certain cleaning procedures and invasive species decals be purchased and displayed. www.ndow.org/Boat/Aquatic_Invasive_Species.

Today's maps report a simple fact. Deep within Canyonlands National Park, the Green River *joins* the Colorado River along its journey to the Gulf of Mexico. But this wasn't always so. In Powell's time, the Colorado River upstream from the confluence to its headwaters was actually called the Grand River. Then, in 1921, Colorado congressman Edward T. Taylor (I wish I had a sassy middle initial) gave an impassioned speech to a congressional committee about renaming the river.

Like most congressmen, the guy had a lot to say. Early river names were applied piecemeal, he argued, by those unfamiliar with distant continuations of the same water body. The name Colorado, given by early Spanish explorers, was surely meant for the entire river, not just the lower portion they visited. It was absurd (absurd!) for one of the world's greatest rivers to have a different name inside its eponymous state. Sure, the Green River was longer above the confluence (730 miles) than the Grand (500 miles), but the latter carried about 25 percent more water to the confluence. (Today, due to water diversions, it's probably even.) And while Taylor didn't quite say the word *Grand* was stupid, he did say it's "merely an adjective . . . Practically everything in Colorado is grand." Despite objections from Wyoming and Utah reps, the resolution passed. Today the Colorado River, at 1,450 miles, is the fifth longest river in the United States.

Regarding names, Colorado means *crimson* or *red* in Spanish and is typically attributed to the reddish color of the silty water, prior to damming, and the red-hued banks along much of its course. The naming of the Green River is more complicated. Anne Zwinger offers a great summary in *Run, River, Run*. Like the Colorado, the Green River had many native names, including *Seedskadee*, meaning river of the prairie hen. These were soon supplanted for Spanish names given by missionaries, like Rio San Buenaventura or Rio Verde. It's been suggested fur trader William Ashely named it for a business pal of his—about as exciting as a market research course on branding concepts. Another option is the green shales and soapstones along the upper river, or just the green color of the water during silty periods—though the river can also run brown or reddish at times. John C. Fremont (okay, I'm getting an initial) believed the name probably came from the strip of vegetation that lines the river's banks in contrast to the surrounding desert.

The renaming of the Colorado is not without controversy. Some folks have claimed Powell started his expeditions on the Green to recognize it as the true main stem of the Colorado River. This claim conveniently ignores the well-documented reason. The railroad went there. The golden spike was nailed only weeks before in Ogden, UT. At the time, it was the only place along the route where heavy boats could be transported from the east. Meanwhile, locals along the Green in Utah are said to ponder how their prospects might have improved if

Grand isn't just an adjective when overlooking Hermit Rapid, found 95 miles downstream from Lees Ferry in Upper Granite Gorge. AMY MARTIN

the river flowing through their impoverished desert communities carried the more famous name. Maybe, but this wistful claim seems to ignore the reality that you can't put wealthy ski resorts in a desert.

Geographic controversies like this are common. Critics (Missourians?) often point to the Mississippi River, noting that from St. Louis to the Gulf, it should have been called the Missouri due to that river's superior length above the confluence. Defenders (Mississippians?) point out that the Mississippi carries more water into the confluence, so *hands off our river name, you jerks*! Go by the water-volume logic, and critics (Ohioans?) point out America's great river should actually be the Ohio.

As is so evident along the Powell route, history is rarely simple. And a town called Colorado River, Utah, doesn't ring as true to me as the dusty river town of Green River, nestled between the dramatic Book Cliffs and the otherworldly folds of the San Rafael Swell. And with all respect to Ohioans, I'm not particularly fond of Huck Finn rafting down the great muddy Ohio River to New Orleans, either.

Water levels and character: Class I–II; gradient averages 3 fpm, and the current is typically moderate at 1–2 mph. The dam releases year-round, and flows can rise substantially during spring melt; current dam operations and links to all valley gauges at www.usbr.gov/uc/water/crsp/cs/ftd.html; USGS Green River below Fontenelle Reservoir: https://waterdata.usgs.gov/wy/nwis/uv?site_no=09211200.

Challenges and safety: Throughout the refuge, occasional rock sills have been placed across the channel for habitat purposes. Slots have been left in the middle to allow for boat passage; less stable paddlers can alternatively portage along shore.

At the museum (there's only one; you'll find it) in Big Piney, WY, I stumbled across a small exhibit about railroad ties. They were cut during winter in the Winds and slid on snow to the Green River, then floated downstream during spring to build the intercontinental railroad that carried Powell's boats to Green River Station in 1869 and 1871.

Boats: Canoe, kayak, SUP, drift boat, raft . . .

Camping: There is no camping allowed inside the refuge. Three campgrounds are available upstream: Tailrace and Weeping Rock right below the dam and Slate Creek at river mile 4.7.

Supplies: The nearest sizable city with groceries and restaurants is Green River, WY; gas and small stores can be found in La Barge and other towns.

Regulations and agency: US Fish & Wildlife Service: www.fws.gov/refuge/Seedska-dee, seedskadee@fws.gov, (307) 875-2187. Fishing regulations and other rules can be found at www.fws.gov/refuge/Seedskadee/visit/rules_and_regulations.html.

Maps: The refuge website offers an excellent river map as PDF for download, which lists access points along 45 river miles through the refuge.

PROLOGUE: "ALL" OF HISTORY BEFORE 1869, WITH APOLOGIES, IN SEVEN PARAGRAPHS

From infinite singularity to ancestral civilizations • conquistadors and missionaries • post–Civil War white expansion • golden spike opportunities

Roughly 13 billion years ago, give or take a few hundred million, the universe was an infinitely dense and infinitely hot singularity—okay, skipping ahead. During the late Pleistocene era, say 50,000 years ago, the fossil records show some human ancestors, including *Homo erectus*, in water-bound places such as Australia, which would have necessitated invention of what we call a boat—even faster? Um, ice age! Bering land bridge. Wooly mammoths. Native populations dispersing across America. Possibly some Vikings did a bit of light sex tourism? A lot of tribes differentiated into complex societies that oscillated between cooperative trading and warfare. Things could be pretty chaotic back then.

Enter Fremont culture, maybe 2,000 years ago. A group of wandering hunters and gatherers, they got curious about some deep and rugged canyons in the Southwest. Who would mess with them down there?

TO
Enterprising Young Men.

THE subscriber wishes to engage ONE HUN-DRED MEN, to ascend the river Missouri to its source, there to be employed for one, two or three years.—For particulars, enquire of Major Andrew Henry, near the Lead Mines, in the County of Washington, (who will ascend with, and command the party) or to the subscriber at St. Louis.
Wm. H. Ashley.
February 13 ——98 tf

A few of these enterprising young men joined Powell on his first expedition, while William Ashley explored upper sections of the route, by boat and by land, during the years before Powell's expeditions.

A diorama, once on display at the South Rim of the Grand Canyon, depicts Spanish conquistador Cárdenas arriving at the Grand Canyon. About the visit, he wrote very little—only that it looked pretty small until his group tried unsuccessfully to reach the river. Neither European nor American explorers would return to the canyon for almost 300 years.

They built small farms on river bottoms and in side canyons. Carried the surplus in decorated pottery up ladders to nice cool granaries they built in the cliffs. Used plant pigments and sharp rocks to create amazing works of art on cliff faces. Built some watchtowers to keep an eye on things and probably also for communication, trade, social gatherings, and religious ceremonies. One day, it stopped raining for what felt like forever. What would everyone eat?

Meanwhile, there was another group to the south, now called Ancestral Puebloans. They did things their own way, had their own sense of style. But much was similar to the Fremont, just happening a bit more to the south, where it was even hotter and more rugged. And one day, it stopped raining again. The ancestral Puebloan culture dispersed, probably into the tribal cultures that existed at the time of the next major arrival.

Spanish conquistadors came, looking for glory and riches in a new world. They believed there was gold everywhere, but clearly the natives were just hiding it or something. The conquistadors acted like gods who had shown up early for an appointment and were pissed. They killed, conquered, enslaved. Many natives died, often from European diseases. Next came missionaries, who were like "Sorry about all those earlier meatheads. Look, we're teachers, and boy, do we have someone we'd like to tell you about. Also, you're doing everything wrong."

Then another type of white European came. They were trappers, or "mountain men," who fancied themselves hunter-gatherers like the natives. Back home, in a smoggy land of factories, there were a ton of rich city folk who craved "authentic things" and would buy basically any type of fur if it was trendy American wilderness

At Museum of the Mountain Man, find exhibits on clothes and tools used by trappers and natives in years before the Powell expeditions.

fur. Meanwhile, a massive war was fought in the young nation over the use of African slave labor in southern states, which led to the emancipation of African Americans and the deaths of 600,000 soldiers, plus many more wounded.

After the war, white settlers moved west in wagons, pretty taken with the whole no rules, no landlords, no taxes stuff. But first they fought the native tribes to stop their "dispersed camping" in every great spot one might want to put a farm or ranch. Eventually, a railroad was built to hasten the postwar settling and create a lucrative real estate market. One retired major, who lost an arm while fighting for the Union side in the Civil War, taught himself a new science called *geology* and used a family connection to get a professor job in Illinois. He started traveling west with students on extended field trips and met a few mountain men. During a trip that visited parts of the Green and Colorado Rivers, an idea came up to explore that big blank spot on the American map.

Wouldn't you know, after years of work, the railroads were getting close to nailing a golden spike. Maybe we can bring in boats? Heard it's a death trap down there. Think we'd end up rich and famous? Don't believe it's ever truly been done. Does a months-long river trip even make sense amid the endless cycle of human atrocity and tragedy? Could be a nice way to get away from it all. How about next May?

The 1869 adventure continues on page 34 . . .

1

FLAMING GORGE RESERVOIR

IF THE GRAND CANYON, OVER 750 RIVER MILES DOWNSTREAM, offers the most sublime paddling along the Powell route, then this first segment—including the official start near Expedition Island and continuing across the impounded waters of Flaming Gorge Reservoir—is the most surreal and anachronistic. Despite this, and in some ways because of it, these roughly 100 miles serve as a worthy destination for short paddling visits or as a challenging proving ground for long-distance Powell pilgrims.

Although the actual historic starting location of the Powell expeditions is down an alley next to a Green River, WY, resident's yard (see page 30), the National Historic Landmark and commemorative info plaques are located just downstream in a lovely landscaped park on a reinforced island near an engineered whitewater kayaking course all worth a visit. The nearby Sweetwater County Museum has great history

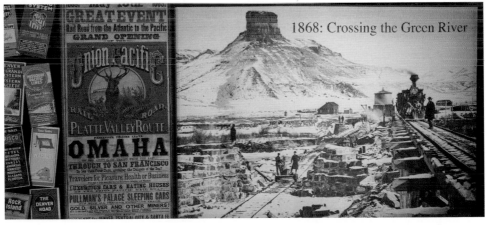

At the Sweetwater County Museum in Green River, WY, you'll find exhibits related to regional history, including the Powell expeditions.

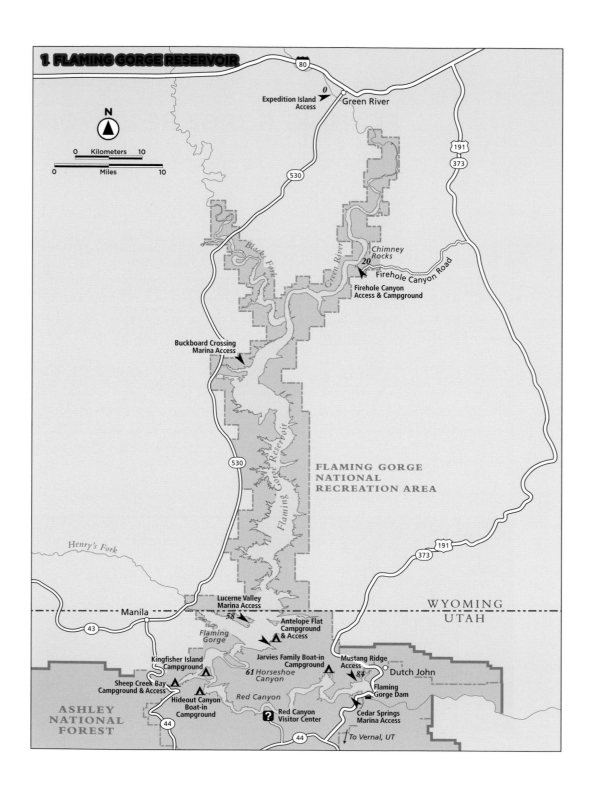

N

Kilometers
0   10

Miles
0   10

Blacks Fork

80

Expedition Island
Access

0

Green River

530

191

373

Green River

*Chimney
Rocks*

20

Firehole Canyon Road

Firehole Canyon
Access & Campground

Buckboard Crossing
Marina Access

530

Flaming Gorge Reservoir

FLAMING GORGE
NATIONAL
RECREATION AREA

Henry's Fork

373 191

Lucerne Valley
Marina Access

Manila

43

58

*Flaming
Gorge*

Antelope Flat
Campground
& Access

WYOMING
UTAH

Kingfisher Island
Campground

Jarvies Family Boat-in
Campground

61 Horseshoe
Canyon

Mustang Ridge
Access

84

Dutch John

Sheep Creek Bay
Campground & Access

Red Canyon

Flaming
Gorge Dam

ASHLEY
NATIONAL
FOREST

Hideout Canyon
Boat-in
Campground

44

?

Red Canyon
Visitor Center

Cedar Springs
Marina Access

44

To Vernal, UT

inside, while outside stands a remarkable statue of John Wesley that indicates the regional importance of the larger-than-life explorer.

For roughly the first 10 miles, paddlers follow a silty and flowing Green River before it's swallowed by a blue-water reservoir that sits incongruously in a desolate high-desert basin for its northern two thirds. South of Firehole Canyon, the lake expands into a series of open bays often wind-whipped. As you continue south, the lake is increasingly patrolled by (a moderate amount) of sport fishermen who use modern sonar systems to chase after record-sized lake trout. And just south of the Utah border, the river enters a series of dramatic canyons—the first of many encountered by Powell's expeditions—which still rise with much of the drama they had during the presettlement era. Plus, you might hear the occasional stereo-blasting party boat on summer weekends.

Still, the lake remains fairly remote and unimpacted. If you only paddle part of this segment, consider either a 2-day trip from Expedition Island to Firehole Canyon for its historic and remote qualities, or explore the four canyons of the southern reservoir—Flaming Gorge, Horseshoe, Kingfisher, and Red. Other than the first 5 or so miles below Green River, WY, the entire segment is within Flaming Gorge National Recreation Area. Primitive camping is allowed most places along the shore (details below), and there are many campgrounds on and off the water.

Duration: To paddle the entire segment will take most paddlers 5 to 7 days, with center-line paddling distance around 85 miles. Depending on weather and skill/comfort, most paddlers often remain closer to shore for safety reasons, which increases the distance paddled.

Access: Through-segment paddlers should start at Expedition Island (N41 31.38' / W109 28.20') and end at Mustang Ridge Boat Launch (N40 55.42' / W109 26.83') or Cedar Springs Marina (N40 54.74' / W109 26.87').

Logistics: All of the official marinas and boat launches allow long-term parking up to 2 weeks in designated lots. For specific information on access points, see the sections below. A self-shuttle for the entire segment takes about 1.25 hours one way, using I-80, US 191, and local roads. Many outfitters offer shuttle services (see sidebar page 24).

Season and weather: Weather around the reservoir can be quite erratic, with thunderstorms, high winds, cold temps, and hail/snow possible at any time of year. Because the river and reservoir can partially ice over during the winter, the suggested seasons to paddle this segment are from midspring to midfall. Lake surface elevation is approximately 6,000'.

"The river is running to the south . . . it glides on in a quiet way as if it thought a mountain range no formidable obstruction. It enters the range by a flaring, brilliant red gorge . . . This is the head of the first of the canyons we are about to explore . . ." —John Wesley Powell

Water level and character: The Green River from town to the reservoir is class I–II with a few gravel bar riffles; water levels from gauge USGS Green River near Green River, WY; reservoir level available at www.usbr.gov/uc/water/crsp/cs/fgd.html.

Challenges and safety: Sudden and rising winds can be a hazard, creating large waves and dangerous conditions on both the open lake and in the narrower canyons. Consider paddling close to shore, and be prepared to seek shelter, which is quite limited on the sparser northern shores. In the open bays, navigation can be challenging given the limited topographic contrast and landmarks; a good map and compass skills are highly recommended.

Boats: For longer lake trips, touring kayaks are preferred to shorter boats, plus canoe, SUP, and . . . raft—legend says it's been done, but should it be done again?

Camping: Be prepared for possible stormy nights. Primitive/dispersed camping is allowed anywhere along the shore following leave-no-trace practices (see pg xxx), except for within 0.25 mile of any administrative site, such as boat ramps, campgrounds, and so on. There are two boat-in campgrounds on the southern reservoir: Hideout Canyon Boat-In Campground has 18 sites and Jarvies Family Boat-In Campground has 8 sites. Both campgrounds are open seasonally from mid-May to mid-September. All sites can be reserved (plus more info available) on recreation.gov. Forty additional drive-in campgrounds are spread throughout the area.

Agencies, regulations, fees: Flaming Gorge National Recreation Area is administered by Ashley National Forest; www.fs.usda.gov/detail/ashley. An entrance fee/receipt or

Setting up camp, one late May, on northern Flaming Gorge Reservoir, an area frequented by afternoon thunderstorms.

Interagency Annual Pass (national parks pass) is required to enter certain areas and must be displayed while parking at some launch locations.

Maps: The US Forest Service publishes a decent and free overview map on the rec area website, which they do not recommend for navigation. A better map is *National Geographic* Waterproof: #704 Flaming Gorge National Recreation Area.

Outfitters: See sidebar below.

Additional Resources: *Lost Canyons of the Green River: The Story Before Flaming Gorge Dam* by Roy Webb.

OUTFITTERS, SERVICES, AND SUPPLIES FOR FLAMING GORGE COUNTRY AND RED CANYON

River Runners Transport, based in Vernal, focuses on Lodore, Yampa, and Deso trips, but they can also help reservoir through-paddlers and those running Red Canyon/Browns Park river segments downstream; (800) 930-7238; www.riverrunnerstransport.com.

Dutch John Resort, located near the dam, is a good choice for paddlers focused on the reservoir and river sections. They offer shuttle services, raft rentals, guided fishing trips for the reservoir and river, cabins, an RV park, tent camping, store, and restaurant; (435) 885-3191; dutchjohnresort.com.

Trout Creek Flies, in Dutch John, is a resort and fishing-focused guide service, also offering raft rentals, shuttles, cabins, lodging, and more; (435) 885-3355; www.troutcreekflies.com.

Flaming Gorge Resort, 10 minutes south of the dam, offers raft/boat rentals, guided fishing trips, shuttles, lodging, RV park, store, and restaurant; (435) 889-3773; www.flaminggorgeresort.com.

Lucerne Valley Marina offers reservoir access, boat rentals (including SUP and kayak), guided trips, floating cabins, camping, store, and restaurant; (435) 784-3483; www.flaminggorge.com.

Cedar Springs Marina offers reservoir access, boat rentals, guided trips, lake tours, a bar & grill, and several campgrounds nearby; (435) 889-3795; www.cedarspringsmarina.com.

Supplies: Green River, WY, in the north, and Vernal, UT, to the south; both offer the most in terms of stores, restaurants, and lodgings. Nearby, towns of Dutch John and Manila, plus area marinas, resorts, and outfitters have stores and restaurants.

Highlights: Expedition Island Park is definitely worth a stop, with plenty of great info plaques and monuments. • The Green River Whitewater Park is found in the main channel next to the island, and the city uses airbags to maintain a surfable feature at different water levels. • About 20 miles down the route, the chimney rocks in Firehole Canyon were the subject of an 1871 expedition photo. • About 30 miles down, Blacks Fork enters from the west and below the reservoirs widens into a series of bays. • About 60 center-line miles down is the dramatic entrance to Flaming Gorge. • One mile in, Horseshoe Canyon starts to the southeast and continues for 4 scenic miles. • Then how about a rainbow amphitheater as you return to Flaming Gorge. • Consider taking a side trip up Sheep Creek Bay if you like flaming geology. • About 70 center-line miles down, Red Canyon starts. • Oh, there's more out there to find!

PADDLING: GREEN RIVER, WY, TO FIREHOLE CANYON

If you want to put-in (very near) where Powell started and float through a stark but intriguing landscape of stacked slate and crumbly buttes mostly unchanged since the original expeditions, then this 22-mile trip is for you. Depending on reservoir levels, you'll have river current for about 10 miles.

Duration: 22 miles; 2 days.

Access: Start at Expedition Island Park in Green River, WY (N41 31.38' / W109 28.20'). There are several access options, so look around before you unload boats. One option is the north shore of the river, in a side channel, just upstream of the 2nd St. bridge. Another option is the downstream tip of the island, near the play feature. Either way, you'll have to carry boats a short way to the water. Regarding parking, you can leave cars overnight in either of two lots. One lot is paved, on the island. The other lot is gravel, just north of the bridge. The Department of Parks & Recreation asks that you inform them if you'll be leaving a vehicle: (307) 872-6151. End at Firehole Canyon boat ramp (N41 21.07' / W109 26.50').

Logistics: A self-shuttle using I-80, US 191, and Flaming Gorge Road (aka FR-106/33) is 33 miles on all paved roads taking 45 minutes one way. See page 24 for shuttle services.

Camping: Once the river enters Flaming Gorge National Recreation Area, primitive camping is allowed along the shore within the rec area. At take-out, there's Firehole Campground.

North and South Chimney Rocks are found in Firehole Canyon, about 20 paddling miles from Expedition Island and the first major landmarks along the route (topographic score!).

PADDLING: FIREHOLE CANYON TO LUCERNE POINT

It's a series of bays! Basically, if you're gonna paddle this section, you might want to do the whole reservoir. Doesn't mean it isn't nice here—it's big and vast and empty. There are few distinct landmarks, so navigation skills are necessary for open water crossings or side cove deviations to stay close to shore. It's the perfect challenge for through-paddling Powell route pilgrims.

Duration: 36+ miles; 2–4 days.

Access: Start at Firehole Canyon boat ramp (N41 21.07' / W109 26.50'). End at Lucerne Valley Marina (N40 59.15' / W109 35.15') or Antelope Flat Marina (N40 57.83' / W109 33.47').

Logistics: A self-shuttle between Firehole and Antelope Flat using US 191 takes a little over 1 hour. Between Firehole and Lucerne Valley, using US 191, I-80, and WY 530 will take 1.5 hours. Shuttle services available (see sidebar page 24).

A topographic relief map of the reservoir, found in the visitor center of Flaming Gorge Dam, which also offers tours of the facility.

PADDLING: FLAMING GORGE TO RED CANYON

The first canyons and significant features encountered by the Powell expeditions are now partially flooded by the reservoir. Gone are Beehive Point and Ashley Falls. But plenty remains above water and is worth visiting. The entry to Flaming Gorge still rises high above lake level. Horseshoe Canyon delivers a jolt of silvery limestone. Hideout Canyon plays across the blue water like piano keys. And upper Red Canyon is still . . . well, it's very red. A few side hikes are possible here and there. You can either primitive camp alongshore or aim for two boat-in campgrounds (see segment details, above).

Duration: 27+ miles; 2–3 days.

A rainbow emerges after a thunderstorm in Hideout Canyon, where Weber sandstone plays across the landscape like piano keys. The white stone often has streaks of desert varnish, a mysterious dark surface oxidation with uncertain origins.

Swooping down off the interstate toward Green River, WY, we hung our heads out the windows of my truck, scanning topography rising on the western side of the river. Our crack team of river detectives included two sleep-deprived paddlers just arrived from St. Louis and Cliff, our transplanted Floridian shuttle driver with a machine gun laugh. Between us, we passed a printout with two historic black-and-white photos taken at the launching spot of the 1871 Powell expedition.

"We're close!" someone shouted, while another pointed northwest toward some distinctive buttes and ridgetops. We zigzagged through dusty streets in a riverside district of warehouses and homes. To the few locals sitting on porches, watching with blank stares, we probably looked like a lost kayak delivery service.

I parked in a dirt lot, and Cliff barreled off down an unpaved riverside alley, like a kid on a scavenger hunt. Our shuttle driver from Dutch John Resort, Cliff had an infectious grin that would give Woz and me a needed boost when picking us up a week later, during a massive storm, and transporting us around Flaming Gorge Dam. I walked along the banks, holding the photo to the horizon. Suddenly, I realized a grading with homes had distorted the landmarks. Was this our spot?

Cliff stopped to chat with the adjacent home owner, who quit weed-whacking and came to his chain-link fence. The fella said the commemorative plaque and accepted starting point was a quarter mile downstream on Expedition Island. But he'd looked at the same picture before and always thought the real launching spot was right here.

After a quick walk to Expedition Island, we confirmed the distinctive buttes were completely out of view. So, we returned to the alleyway where the visuals aligned, and in late May, 146 years and a few days after Powell, we launched our Pyranha Fusion kayaks for our 150-mile trip.

At the time, I didn't consider this minor "discovery" to have much significance. Coming to the route from afar, I'd just assumed Expedition Island was a symbolic

Even commemorative depictions of Powell's boats seem to leak.

If they try to put another monument on Expedition Island, some fear the whole island will sink.

landmark. But 2 years later, I returned to visit David, a historian at Sweetwater County Museum. When I casually mentioned my observation, he drifted off before giving me a curiously wild look.

"I've seen those photos," he said. "Will you follow me?"

Soon, David was driving through the same riverside district, scanning the topography. He parked near the alleyway and led me right to the spot from which Woz and I had launched over 2 years before.

"The moment you said that, it hit me like a jolt." David stared up at the bluffs. "Who starts an expedition from an island? There was no bridge in 1869."

David explained that, these days, it's become commonplace around town and in modern history books to describe both expeditions as launching from the island. Having read the original accounts, I can report nothing about an island launch is recorded about either expedition. In a July 3 letter to the *Chicago Evening Journal*, Powell described the boats being loaded with freight and then launched. This freight would have totaled many thousands of pounds. I guess one could theorize they loaded up and moved the boats to an island, in the middle of a river rising from spring flows, so they could go get drunk in town? But if so, why didn't they leave until 2 p.m. the next day? Even hungover modern river runners can load up and get moving faster than that! These were mountain men. In *A Canyon Voyage*, Dellenbaugh was more detailed about the 1871 launch, describing a little cove on river-left, downstream from the railroad.

Perhaps the confusion comes from a highly visible 1949 monument, placed in the exact center of the island, which declares, "Marking the spot from which John Wesley Powell and party departed . . ." National Historic Landmark status was conferred in 1968, leading to a 1969 monument, located at the northern tip of the island. Possibly attempting to subtly correct any confusion, this monument is within sight of the actual starting spot and is more vague, mentioning Powell launched from "these environs." A minor controversy, sure, but still a curious little mystery—just one of many along the Powell route.

Access: Starting at Antelope Flat Marina (N40 59.15' / W109 35.15') and ending at Mustang Ridge Boat Launch (N40 55.42' / W109 26.83') is recommended due to a much shorter shuttle. You can also start at Lucerne Valley Marina (N40 59.15' / W109 35.15') and end at Cedar Springs Marina (N40 54.74' / W109 26.87'), or some other combination. Paddlers can also be picked up or start/end day trips at the Flaming Gorge Dam Visitor Center, but that lot only offers daytime parking.

Logistics: A self-shuttle between Antelope Flat and Mustang Ridge, using Antelope Flat Rd./FR 145, US 191, and Mustang Ridge Rd./FR 184, will take 20 minutes one way. Between Lucerne Valley Marina and Cedar Springs Marina, using WY 530, UT 43, UT 44, and US 191, it takes 1 hour one way.

OTHER PADDLING: FLAMING GORGE WATER TRAILS

In recent years, the Flaming Gorge Chamber of Commerce has been encouraging short paddling day trips by kayak or SUP. Several water-trail routes depart from various access points, such as Sheep Creek, Cedar Springs, and Mustang Ridge. The chamber has published maps on their website of the routes, which explore various side channels and reservoir areas with lower motor boat traffic. Visit www.flaminggorge country.com/paddling.

Sheep Creek Bay, in the bottom half of the photo, proves that even the side arms of Flaming Gorge Reservoir are worth exploring.

A lot of people still look up to John Wesley Powell, especially in front of the Sweetwater County Museum. But dude wasn't actually 20 feet tall. This statue not to scale.

1869, PART I: THOSE EARLY, CAREFREE DAYS NEAR FLAMING GORGE

A lot of blank spots here • goodbye! (forever) • foreshadows of disaster • the first canyons • JWP's triangulation face

On May 24, John Wesley Powell arrived on the recently completed railroad at a dusty Wyoming outpost of riverside shacks beneath a stark landscape of buttes and ridges. To Green River Station, Powell brought crates of equipment, rations donated by the War Department, four big wooden rowboats, and a goal to explore the last blank spot on the American map. Waiting for him was a ragtag crew of mountain men and ex-soldiers. None of these dudes had ever run a whitewater rapid, but they were preparing for the challenge like modern raft guides—by filling their own blank spots with every ounce of whiskey they could find.

The next morning, the crew felt a bit foggy while loading the boats on shore, as described by Jack Sumner, an ex-soldier turned mountain man who became lead boatman in Powell's pilot craft, the *Emma Dean*. A few townspeople came down to the river to say goodbye (forever) to these hard-partying nutcases who were led by a serious one-armed Civil War major who was 35 years old and talked like a Victorian aristocrat. Said they were going a thousand miles all the way through the Grand Canyon? But everyone knew that river dropped over sheer waterfalls before plunging into the depths of the earth. A few townswomen may have crossed themselves and blessed these poor souls. A few townsmen may have called them *idiots* under their breaths, with a mixture of relief and regret they hadn't been asked to come along.

The early days down the river were pretty fun. Sometimes boats ran aground on sandbars, and the men flopped in the water to push them off. Expedition camps were made in the willows. They gathered driftwood for fires and explored a barren landscape faintly dusted by spring grasses. Some of the men chased bighorn sheep with rifles. They usually failed but occasionally got one for dinner. When the cook, a 20-year-old mountain man named Hawkins, alone carried in a sheep on day 2, the others teased that he must have found it dead. Meanwhile, Powell scrambled around with a few men, looking for fossils amid crumbly slate formations, which the major thought resembled architectural forms and strange statues.

As the ten men in four boats progressed downriver, the bulk of the Uinta Mountains grew in the distance. There were occasional miscommunications between boats. Rowing the second boat, *Maid of the Cañon*, was George Bradley. He was a 32-year-old active sergeant from Massachusetts, who wrote the most thorough and complete journal of the entire expedition. In exchange for contributing his relevant experience in geology and running ocean fishing boats, Powell had arranged for his discharge from the US Army. Joining Bradley was Powell's younger brother, Walter, a former prisoner of war in South Carolina with lingering temper issues. On the second day, Bradley noted the pilot boat signaled danger, but he and Walter, "supposing it to be only a small rapid, did not obey immediately and in consequence [their boat] was caught on a shoal." A minor incident, but one which foreshadowed later calamities.

As they moved south, Powell describes—in limited journal entries, plus his 1875 published account—a brilliant red gorge, about 20 miles distant, where the river dramatically entered a mountain range. But first, a few miles upstream at Henrys Fork, the men retrieved a hidden gear cache brought in overland a few months before. Here it's worth mentioning an occasional misconception about the expeditions. While the southern parts of the route—especially the rugged Grand Canyon—were mostly unexplored by Americans, much of the canyons, basins, and Native American tribes

The boats used on the 1871–72 Powell expedition wait for launch from Green River Station; E. O. Beaman. US GEOLOGICAL SURVEY

Brick buildings in Green River Station abandoned after railroad construction, as seen in 1871; E. O. Beaman. US GEOLOGICAL SURVEY

An early camp of the second Powell expedition at Flaming Gorge in 1871; E. O. Beaman.
US GEOLOGICAL SURVEY

above Marble Canyon were in country known to white Americans through exploration and trapping.

Inside what they named Flaming Gorge, the river entered periodic chutes and rapids as the current hastened. The boats often shipped (or filled with) water and were bailed in eddies below. Rowing the third boat, *No Name*, was Oramel Howland. At age 36, he was the oldest man on the expedition, one of only four crewmen to not serve in the Civil War. With experience as a mountain guide and newspaperman in Denver, Oramel's job was to prepare maps from their surveys. In one of two highly detailed letters to *Rocky Mountain News*, Oramel wrote those first descents felt like railroad speeds of 60 miles per hour, adding this would come to feel slow compared to later rapids. This tendency to exaggerate speeds, distances, elevations, and experiences was a common theme throughout all journals and later accounts of the expedition—especially John Wesley's. Thus, all subsequent retellings, including this one, involve a great deal of interpretation as they try to unravel fact and fiction. Basically, these men were natural whitewater boaters—certainly in their bravado and confidence, even if raw in the river-running skills.

The river soon wound into Horseshoe Canyon, carving through startling white formations of limestone and shale. Then came Kingfisher Canyon, where swallows swarmed like bees around nests tucked into cracks of a rock dome that resembled a straw beehive. Today, Beehive Point is mostly a forgotten name on a map, and paddlers may only float above the landmark buried beneath Flaming Gorge Reservoir.

Next was Red Canyon, with sheer sandstone walls, where the crew labored over the first few of about 100 portages and linings around increasingly challenging rapids. Here, Powell made a quirky discovery that may help distinguish his personality from most of the crewmen. As he'd been coming down the river, sitting in his armchair lashed to the deck of the *Emma Dean*, the major noticed how his perspective of approaching mountains shifted. When viewed straight on, the inclination of the oncoming slope appeared to be excessively steep and the overall height seemed shorter. Not until the river passed beside the mountain did the true slope reveal itself.

Somehow, Powell decided if he lay on his side, the triangulating effect between his two eyes allowed him a baseline to better estimate the true elevation of a summit. While the triangulation aspect seems questionable, Powell's method of seeing the landscape anew has merit. By lying down to change his perspective, Powell may have found that the altered vantage point helped him estimate topographic elevations. It's a method not unlike visual analysis techniques, where students are encouraged to rotate an image to help notice the details. Regardless, it's somewhat comical to imagine that while Powell's men were charging across the landscape after sheep, portaging massive rowboats around rapids, and eventually going hungry as rations diminished, they might have looked over and seen John Wesley lying on his side in camp, staring sideways at mountainsides, and jotting notes about topographic observations.

The 1869 adventure continues on page 56 . . .

RED CANYON AND BROWNS PARK

LIKE A MICROCOSM FOR THE ENTIRE POWELL ROUTE, this 47-mile segment balances two high-profile whitewater sections with a pair of slow-moving but scenic stretches that see little traffic. Just below Flaming Gorge Dam, the wildly popular A Section attracts fly fishermen from around the world, who stalk cold, clear waters for rainbow, cutthroat, and brown trout—often from guided drift boats. Much of the 7 miles is through the narrow remnants of Red Canyon. Near Little Hole, the canyon widens until the river joins the vast Browns Park. The Little Hole National Recreation Trail (yes, that's a thing) follows the left bank, including many boardwalk segments, for the entire 7 miles. The trail offers hikers and anglers another way to experience a remarkable gorge, where pine forest clings to crimson bedrock.

Rental rafts and inflatable kayaks are common in A Section, especially summer weekend afternoons, which can see periodic party flotillas. The pool drop rapids are easy class II, the current is swift, and camping is not allowed—all making for a rewarding day trip. Some paddlers will prefer quieter times, such as early morning, midweek, or shoulder seasons. However you plan it, Powell paddlers should not miss this section.

Below Little Hole Rec Area, B Section is a little over 8 miles of easy class II and this segment's the second most popular run among day fishermen and overnight paddlers. It's a bit more remote, a bit less crowded, and there are 17 riverside campsites. Most of the river-left sites can be reached by an unofficial trail, while river-right sites are boat-in. Some sites can be reserved online, while others require a sign-up in person at Little Hole. Together, A and B Sections make for a great 2-day trip.

Next comes the slower C Section, which includes a scenic bonus through intimate Swallow Canyon. Near the Colorado state line, the river becomes increasingly sluggish. Paddlers will likely see more bald eagles than people in Browns Park National Wildlife Refuge. Due to the remote location, far removed from the tourist hubs around Flaming Gorge Dam, these two sections are little paddled. Overgrown tamarisk can make camping a challenge, but several worn-in spots and a few campgrounds will aid ambitious through-paddlers.

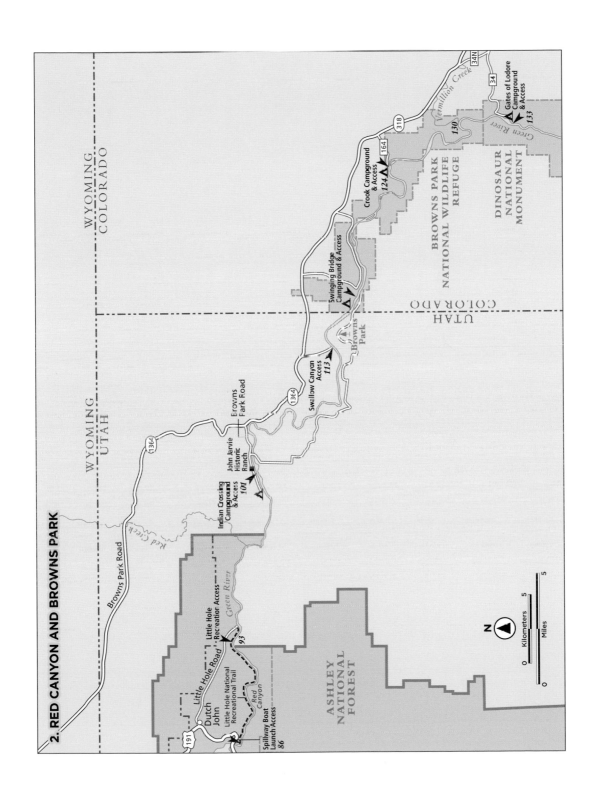

2. RED CANYON AND BROWNS PARK

WYOMING
COLORADO

WYOMING
UTAH

UTAH
COLORADO

Browns Park Road

Red Creek

1364

1364

Browns Park Road

Little Hole Road

Little Hole National Recreational Trail

Dutch John

191

93

Spillway Boat Launch Access *86*

Little Hole Recreation Access

Green River

Red Canyon

ASHLEY NATIONAL FOREST

Indian Crossing Campground & Access *101*

John Jarvie Historic Ranch

Browns Park Road

Swallow Canyon Access *113*

Browns Park

Swinging Bridge Campground & Access

Crook Campground & Access *124*

164

318

130

Vermillion Creek

Green River

34N

34

Gates of Lodore Campground & Access *133*

BROWNS PARK NATIONAL WILDLIFE REFUGE

DINOSAUR NATIONAL MONUMENT

N

0   5 Kilometers
0   5 Miles

Like phantoms from Powell's time, modern fishing drift boats ply the trout-filled waters of Red Canyon below Flaming Gorge Dam. Like a photographic stalker, I jumped out of the bushes on the trail through A Section to snap this picture.

Continuing into Dinosaur National Monument by river offers engaging views of the dramatically rising Gates of Lodore, but realize that this marks the start of a permitted segment involving one of the hardest lotteries to win along the entire Powell route.

Duration: The entire segment is 47 miles, and through-paddling will take 3–5 days.

Access: Through-paddlers should start at Spillway Boat Launch (W40 54.52' / N109 25.34') and end at Gates of Lodore boat ramp (W40 43.64' / N108 53.30'), unless possessing a permit to continue.

Logistics: A self-shuttle between Spillway and Gates of Lodore, using US 191, Browns Park Rd., CO 318, and County Rd. 34N/34, is 60 miles and will take 1.5 hours one way. Cars may be parked overnight at both locations. Shuttle services are available (see page 24).

Season and weather: Spring–fall; because of the constant releases from Flaming Gorge Dam, the river typically does not freeze over on this stretch, so you could probably get through in winter. At all times of year, rain is possible here. Elevation at Indian Springs/John Jarvie Ranch is around 5,500'.

Water level and character: This starts as a class II run (9 fpm) through A and B Sections, with one class III rapid at Red Creek before becoming very, very class I. Flaming Gorge Dam releases continuous minimum flows of 800 cfs, meaning there's always enough water for most boats; high flows in the spring can reach 4,000–5,000 cfs—even more during high-water years—increasing the difficulty and skills needed for A and B. Releases from Flaming Gorge Dam here: www .usbr.gov/uc/water/crsp/cs/fgd.html; the gauge below the dam is USGS Green River near Greendale, UT.

Challenges and safety: A Section can get pretty crowded in peak season or become a party float on some weekends. Watch out for the low bridge in C Section, details below.

Boats: Raft, drift boat, and ducky are most common for A Section, but whitewater kayak, SUP, and canoe would be fun for experienced paddlers; use any boat from C Section and down.

Camping: No camping in A Section. Camping in B Section by reserved site (see below). Camping in C Section is dispersed, but due to tamarisk overgrowth, you'll want to find etched-in spots. Camp only in official campgrounds in the wildlife refuge.

Agencies, regulations, fees: And how! Ashley National Forest manages A, B, C Sections jointly with BLM; Vernal, UT, field office; (435) 789-1181; fs.usda.gov/Ashley. Fees charged for Spillway and Little Hole access points; Interagency Annual Pass (aka National Parks Pass) is accepted. At Spillway access, there is an upper parking lot that's free, which provides trail access to the river. Camping requires portable toilet system. Browns Park National Wildlife Refuge; (970) 365-3613; www.fws.gov/refuge/browns_park. Dinosaur National Monument, see segment 3 for info.

> " . . . ALL ABOARD, AND OFF WE GO DOWN THE . . . BEAUTIFUL RIVER THAT INCREASES ITS SPEED . . . WE RUN THROUGH WAVES AT EXPRESS SPEED . . . THE BOATS BOUNDING THROUGH WAVES LIKE A SCHOOL OF PORPOISE . . . WE PLUNGE ALONG, SINGING, YELLING, LIKE DRUNKEN SAILORS, ALL FEELING THAT SUCH RIDES DO NOT COME EVERY DAY."
> —*Jack Sumner, 1869*

A pair of hikers descends toward the Little Hole National Recreation Trail, which parallels the river for 7 miles through A Section.

Permits: The only permit for this segment is a day "play" permit from Dinosaur National Monument, to float in to the monument and take-out at Gates of Lodore; info on their website.

Maps: The best topographic river maps for this segment are in *Belknap's Waterproof Dinosaur River Guide*.

Outfitters and services: See local resorts on page 24; plus two raft companies offer guided trips.

Dinosaur River Expeditions offers guided raft trips for 1–3 days through Red Canyon and Browns Park; (800) 345-7238; www.dinosaurriverexpeditions.com.

OARS offers guided raft trips for 1–3 days through Red Canyon and Browns Park; (800) 346-6277; www.oars.com.

Highlights: As usual, much to report here. The first few miles in Red Canyon have a half dozen class II–II+ rapids with a dozen names. • Camping in the widening canyon of B Section is a real treat. • About 97 miles down the modern Powell route, Red Creek Rapid is the first significant class III. • Near Indian Crossing access, which divides B and C Sections, the John Jarvie Historic Ranch is a great riverside attraction, with original buildings, replica store, a garden, and lots of trinkets from a forgotten era (the small museum is typically open business hours Tues through Sat, but call to check: 435-885-3307. • Near the end of C Section, the river dips back into the mountains through Swallow Canyon, a real bonus. • Utah-Colorado border is reported by the cutest sign in willows, and the police boats should stop following you around here. • Swinging Bridge has a gaping hole from the time a guy accidentally drove a tractor across. • Browns Park National Wildlife Refuge has almost too much birdlife— quit bald eagle bragging, BPNWR. • Vermillion Creek enters from left about 130 miles down the route, the site of some 1871 side explorations and photography. • Approaching the Gates of Lodore from afar is one of the biggest highlights. Going through them? Even better.

PADDLING: FLAMING GORGE DAM TO LITTLE HOLE (A SECTION)

Great scenery, lovely water, excellent fishing, consistent flows, adjective adjective et cetera. . . . Everyone loves this section—and for good reason. Who are you to defy *everyone*? But, seriously, don't be scared off by the chance of crowds. Late spring, early fall, summer weekdays, mornings, early evenings. Chances are you'll see some people, but you won't see *all* of the people. And try to take your time, if you can.

A lot of greenery in Red Canyon, fun class II rapids, and, with a riverside trail, a perfect place for a packrafting run in my Kokopelli Nirvana. INA SEETHALER

If you need shuttle services or want to rent boats for a self-guided trip, options are available from local resorts and outfitters listed for Flaming Gorge Country on page 24. And there are a few companies offering guided trips, listed below.

Duration: 7 miles; 2.5–4+ hours; many groups, especially guided fly-fishing trips, take their sweet, sweet time in A Section by hitting every eddy.

Access: Put-in at the paved ramp at Spillway Boat Launch (W40 54.52' / N109 25.34'), just downstream from Flaming Gorge Dam. Take-out at any of the three paved boat ramps at Little Hole Recreation Area (W40 54.65' / N109 18.91').

Logistics: A self-shuttle using (creative name!) Spillway Boat Launch Rd., US 191, and Little Hole Rd. is 10 miles and 20 minutes one way. Note that Spillway Boat Ramp is a small and often busy spot. Vehicles are allowed only 10 minutes to stop and launch boats; outfitters and most private boaters use boat trailers. Two upper parking lots are available for prepping boats and day-use parking. A short but steep trail leads between the parking lots and the launching area.

"The sweet songs of birds, the fragrant odor of wild roses, the low, sweet rippling of the ever murmuring river at sunrise in the wilderness, made everything as lovely as a poet's dream." —Jack Sumner

Water level and character: Details on character, boats, and so on above; A Section is the hardest class II section in this segment, maybe bordering on II+ at certain flows.

PADDLING: LITTLE HOLE TO INDIAN CROSSING (B SECTION)

The scenery isn't as impressive, but it's still very nice throughout this cleverly named section, brought to paddlers by the letter B. Side hikes are possible in many places along the valley slopes. Red Creek Rapid—okay, we get it, the geology is *very* red!—offers a fun challenge, being the only significant rapid above Lodore that remains along the Powell route. Fishing is great, camping is great, the Jarvie Historic Ranch near take-out is great. Less great is the longer shuttle, but the run makes it well worth your time.

Duration: 8.25 miles; 4–6 hours or camp overnight.

Access: Put-in at the paved boat ramp at Little Hole Recreation Area (W40 54.65' / N109 18.91'). Take-out at the gravel boat ramp at Indian Crossing Boat Launch (W40 53.82' / N109 11.12').

If you're paddling through an empty valley in the mountain west and you come across a sign pointing to "graves," you should usually get out of there. Unless it's the Jarvie Historic Ranch just below the start of C Section, about 102 paddling miles down the route.

Logistics: A self-shuttle using Little Hole Rd., US 191, Browns Park Rd. (aka UT 1364), and Indian Crossing Boat Launch Rd. is 37 miles and 1 hour each way. Many outfitters offer shuttle services (see sidebar page 24).

Camping: There are 17 primitive riverside campsites available in B Section, following a complicated reservation system. During the high season (mid-Apr to end of Sept) six sites can be reserved and paid for online at www.recreation.gov under Green River Float-In Campsites, UT. The remaining 11 sites must be reserved in person using the camp registration board, with cash payment, at Little Hole Rec Area. While some materials suggest this can be done only by walk-up the day of your stay, many boaters stop by and sign up in advance for camping dates later that week. During low season, all sites are walk-in, meaning no sign-up or payment is necessary—just occupy the site. The site names are posted on riverside signs, and there's a map on recreation.gov site. Vault toilets can be found near Cottonwood Camp and Red Creek Camps; however, the forest service requires boaters to bring an approved portable toilet system for all sites. BLM manages Indian Creek Campground, with 22 drive-up sites, no reservations, at the take-out. Water is available—a good place for through-paddlers to fill up.

Water level and character: More in segment details, above, but know that B Section is easier than A, with less frequent rapids, but still class II, with one class III at Red Creek.

PADDLING: INDIAN CROSSING TO SWALLOW CANYON (C SECTION)

C Section is—wait for it—above average (rimshot, cymbal crash). Supposedly the stretch used to be more popular among fishermen and overnight paddlers but fell out of favor over the years. Two reasons may be the remote location from the hub surrounding Flaming Gorge Dam and the overgrown tamarisk, which has rendered most riverside camps inaccessible to boaters. The result is an empty and open western feel that can no longer be found in many places along the route. Plus, two bonuses: The John Jarvie Historic Ranch is on river-left, 0.5 mile below put-in. Later, just as the river seems to have left all canyons astern, it makes a surprising dip south into the Uinta Mountains for 2 miles through Swallow Canyon. In there, up-canyon winds can be tricky—but who paddles the Powell route because it's easy? In other words, you may have C Section to yourself. Enjoy.

This is a windmill.

"We start early and run through to Brown's Park. Halfway down the valley, a spur of a red mountain stretches across the river, which cuts a canyon through it. Here the walls are comparatively low, but vertical. A vast number of swallows have built their adobe houses on the face of the cliffs." —John Wesley Powell (Located about 110 paddling miles down the route.)

Duration: 11.5 miles; 5–8 hours or camp overnight.

Access: Start at Indian Crossing boat ramp (W40 53.82' / N109 11.12'). End at Swallow Canyon boat ramp (W40 50.65' / N109 4.94').

Logistics: You might be able to arrange a shuttle through Flaming Gorge area outfitters, especially if you're coming down from upper sections. Otherwise, it's a self-shuttle for 9 miles and 20 minutes using Browns Park Rd., UT 1364, and Swallow Canyon River Access Road.

Challenges and safety: Less than 1 mile from put-in, Taylor Flat Bridge is a low bridge that becomes dangerous at higher water levels. Several paddlers have drowned here over the years. Approach with caution and portage on river-right using the boat

I snapped awake on a brisk morning in early June at the head of Swallow Canyon near Browns Park. It was day 9, on our way down from Green River, WY, and something wasn't right. The backs of my hands had rashed over—red, bumpy, and itching. I thought back to night 7, camping in B Section. For a fire, I'd collected branches that had been cut and abandoned by previous paddlers. The timing was about right. *Shit*, I chided myself. *Do I have poison ivy on my hands?*

As we continued downstream that day and the irritation worsened, I began to have doubts. The rash hadn't spread beyond a limited patch between my wrists and first interphalangeal joints. The previous week, while kayaking across Flaming Gorge Reservoir, I sunburned my hands in the exact same spot. I'd alternated between slathering on zinc oxide sunscreen and wearing neoprene paddling gloves, which I regularly dipped in water to cool. Consulting the medical book in my first-aid kit, I discovered an alternate diagnosis I'd never experienced. *Prickly heat*, aka heat rash, when the pores clog and sweat is trapped beneath the skin. In my attempts to limit the sunburn, I'd inadvertently made my hands worse by using two nonbreathable remedies.

This initial injury, though minor, foretold a string of misfortune that followed my hands along the Powell route like a disaster movie montage. No, my hands weren't shot, stabbed, or infected with malaria. Just felt like it sometimes.

Fingers jammed against cam buckles. Open blisters from paddle rub. Rope burns from runaway bow lines. Blood blisters from closing cooler lids. Cracked creases from freeze-thaw action. Windburn from up-canyon gusters. Hand cramps from overuse. Bites from black fly swarms. Impalements from slate rock. Second-degree burns from stove mishaps. Splinters from materials that I did not know could splinter. Smashed fingernails, split fingernails, torn fingernails. Hangnails that make grown men cry.

At one point, during a winter Grand Canyon trip, I had so many cracks, I couldn't bend my right index finger for 3 days. "What are you pointing at?" my buddy teased me. Then he glanced at his own hands. "Oh, I'm bleeding."

Another day, another friend jokingly sprinted away from camp, shouting, "Keep your damn hand sanitizer away from me!" The alcohol-based jelly might be great for sanitizing, but it's dehydrating murder on damaged hands. That was one lesson learned among many. Over time, our hands toughened while we adapted to the constantly changing conditions—cold, hot, freezing, thawing, sunny, rainy, sandy, windy. Conditions that can be particularly tough on paddlers coming from more humid climates or an office.

Some used only biodegradable soaps instead of sanitizer. Some used Working Hands creams, waxes, or moisturizing lotions. Meticulous nail care—we're talking boat-based salon-type stuff. Water-based sunscreens in addition to zinc. And

Adventure photographer Forest Woodward captures a never-ending topic of commiseration along the Powell route. FOREST WOODWARD

because I'm so fair and even my hand tan vanishes each winter, I picked up a set of sun clothes that included light, breathable paddling gloves for peak brightness hours. Some bring work gloves for rigging rafts and gathering firewood. None of this solves the challenges that affect paddlers' hands along the Powell route, but it certainly mitigates some of the pain. And for the rest, luckily there's beer—just don't cut yourself opening the tab.

ramp to Bridge Hollow Campground, a BLM fee area with 14 drive-in sites and potable water.

Camping: Other than the campgrounds at put-in and Taylor Flat Bridge, it's dispersed down here, and the old designated sites have overgrown, so look for etched-in sites made by more recent boaters.

PADDLING: BROWNS PARK NATIONAL WILDLIFE REFUGE

Bald eagle families perched in stilt nests. Lazy meanders where the current is not moving upstream, but I understand where you're coming from. And a broken bridge with a gaping hole where an oversized tractor broke through in recent years. Browns Park is quintessential drop-off-the-map Powell route Americana.

Duration: 4, 11.5, or 20 miles possible; 2–3, 4–6, or 6–10 hours/overnight.

Access: Start at Swallow Canyon boat ramp (W40 50.65' / N109 4.94'). The next access, 4 river miles downstream, is a gravel ramp on river-left at Swinging Bridge Campground (W40 49.82' / N109 2.21'). The lowest access in the wildlife refuge, 11.5 miles from Swallow Canyon, is a gravel (or mud) ramp on river-left at Crook Campground (W40 48.51' / N108 55.54'). The final access point for this segment, 20 river miles from Swallow, is in Dinosaur National Monument at Gates of Lodore boat ramp (W40 43.64' / N108 53.30').

Logistics: Self-shuttle uses Swallow Canyon River Access Road to UT 1364/CO 318. For Swinging Bridge, 20 minutes total, head south on CR 83. For Crook Campground, 30 minutes total, head south on CR 164. For Gates of Lodore, 40 minutes total, turn south on CR 34N to 34, and you're there.

Camping: In the official campgrounds at Swinging Bridge and Crook only.

Regulations, agencies, fees: More details above, but keep in mind you need the "play" permit from Dino to enter the monument.

Supplies and services: You're just kidding, right? Plan ahead.

A family of bald eagles in a stilt nest inside Browns Park National Wildlife Refuge. You won't miss them if you blink. Slow current, fair warning.

1869, PART II: WELL, IT WASN'T NAMED DISASTER FALLS OUT OF IRONY

An oh-shit moment at Ashley Falls • a portal to glory or gloom? • yeah, it's looking like the latter, boss • okay, who brought the whiskey?

In Red Canyon came several firsts for the expedition, including a system for lining certain rapids. While some men on shore used ropes to lower a boat downriver, one or two others stayed in that boat and used oars to push around the rocks. Next came a lesson in portaging at Ashley Falls, today covered by the reservoir, named by the men for a fur trapping company owner who explored the Green River in buffalo-skin boats years before.

Powell's four boats stopped against cliffs on river-right, just upstream from a steep drop where a massive house boulder rose from the river. There was an open chute on river-left, but it seemed to plunge too deeply to chance a fully loaded run. Meanwhile, the left shore looked rugged but passable for carrying supplies. It was an *oh-shit* moment common among modern exploratory whitewater descents—the boats were on the wrong side of the river above a portage.

To get across, Sumner and wild-haired mountain man Bill Dunn began a series of daring crossings above the falls, using the smaller and lighter pinewood pilot boat to ferry batches of gear to shore. Once the larger and heavier freight boats, made of oak, had been relieved of half their 2,000-pound loads, all boats made the ferry. Descending the falls involved the rest of the day and much of the next, portaging about 7,000 pounds of gear across the boulder-strewn left bank. Then they lined the empty boats.

Below Ashley Falls, frequent whitewater continued, which exhilarated the men. Bradley noted these rapids were "more noisy today than yesterday but the [boulders] have not been so thick." During the descent of Red Canyon, including what today is called A and B Sections, a process developed. The *Emma Dean* would strike out ahead, probe the rapid, and eddy out below. Then Powell would wave a signal flag to direct the heavier boats. In this way, the expedition rowed out from Red Canyon into the wide expanse of Browns Park on the afternoon of June 2, 100 miles and 10 days down from Green River Station.

The expedition spent four leisurely days traversing the high desert valley. While the hunters returned empty-handed from following the frequent tracks of deer and bighorn sheep, other pursuits were more successful. Powell shot two grouse, which were fried for breakfast the next morning. Bradley caught a dozen mountain whitefish and a few native suckers, possibly a type of chub that's endangered today. In Sumner's journal, the second longest recorded during the expedition, he compared eating the former to pork, while the latter was like chewing on a paper sheath of sewing needles.

Crew from the second expedition line boats past Ashley Falls in Red Canyon; E. O. Beaman. US GEOLOGICAL SURVEY

Further down the valley, the men rowed past two prospectors in a boat who had come down the river from Green River Station a few days ahead of the expedition. Onward, through Swallow Canyon and into what today is a wildlife refuge. Here some ducks and a goose were shot, plus more fish were caught by Powell and Hall. Throughout the valley, the men conducted off-river surveys. Oramel Howland drew up a map. His younger brother, Seneca, plus Bradley and Hall, measured a geologic section on the northeast side of the river. Powell and Dunn twice explored together on foot.

First, they ascended a hilly hogback to the south, with Powell following the ridge and Dunn ascending the gulch. On top, Powell viewed the river winding its way through the valley before turning south back into the Uintas. As they continued downriver, two hulky mountains rose like gate posts on either side of the river. The men proceeded until camping just upstream, on the left shore, not far from today's Gates of Lodore campground. Dunn and Powell climbed about 2,000 feet to the summit of the eastern canyon wall, which he described as "buttressed on a grand scale." Powell noted how the river filled the channel from wall to wall. How the gates resembled an opening to a region of glory. Or, how, as the sun set and the shadows rose, it became more of a portal to a darkening region of gloom.

The expedition started into the Canyon of Lodore the next morning, encountering increasingly challenging rapids. In one spot, they reached a foaming cataract, possibly Winnie's Rock, and lined the boats past. Below, frequent rapids continued until 1 p.m., when the *Emma Dean* pulled to shore on river-left above what Bradley described as the "wildest rapid yet seen." Powell signaled to the others to eddy out, and two of the freight boats made the landing. But the *No Name* was not so lucky.

Rower Oramel later wrote the *No Name* failed the landing due to misunderstanding Powell's signal plus the heaviness of their boat due to shipped water. Sumner noted the *No Name* was farther out in the current than the others, but they tried their hardest to make the left shore. Realizing their hopeless situation, the three men in the *No Name* turned into the most daunting rapid yet encountered—a series of chutes, waves, and holes through a channel pocked by exposed boulders.

Their new aim was to run ashore, mid-rapid, but the *No Name* hit a rock, spun sideways, and took on even more water. Two men were thrown overboard, but they clung to the boat and flopped back in. More rocks were struck, which gouged a hole in the forward planks. Thrown overboard was Frank Goodman, an English traveler who joined the expedition at Green River Station a few days before launch and possibly paid Powell for the ticket. Now, Goodman swam for the top of a midchannel island, but he was swept downstream and soon clung for dear life to a barrel-sized boulder.

The *No Name* was 6 inches underwater and moving downstream through a swift riffle. Off to the left was a gravel bar island. Downstream were more big rapids like those above. Oramel yelled to Seneca to jump. The two men leapt toward the island, crawling onshore a hundred feet apart. Spotting Goodman, who was calling for help, Oramel pulled a long root from a driftwood pile. Scrambling upstream 50 feet, Oramel used the root like an outstretched paddle or modern throw-rope to pull Goodman onto the island.

Reunited, it may have seemed like a stable situation—except for one thing. The three men stood on a shallow midchannel gravel bar, today called No Name Island. It was springtime, and the river was rising. Within hours, they feared the gravel bar itself might be part of the river. The men built a small fire against a downed tree and waited for help.

Upstream, the other men had watched the chaos as the *No Name* crashed through the rapid. All three were swimming by the time it swept out of sight around the corner. Some of the men on shore, including Powell, scrambled down the left in chase. Jack Sumner, meanwhile, hatched a plan with a few others. The lighter *Emma Dean* was unloaded on shore and lowered by ropes until it was across from No Name Island. Then, Sumner, or the trapper, as he referred to himself, launched into the rapid and

The Gates of Lodore as they appeared in 1871;
weren't too different from today. J. K. Hillers.
US GEOLOGICAL SURVEY

Disaster Falls in the Canyon of Lodore, as encountered by the second Powell expedition; J. K. Hillers. US GEOLOGICAL SURVEY

ferried to the rescue. To depart the island, the three men waded the boat upstream of the island, through shallow shoals, to ferry back to the river-left shore.

Once regrouped on shore, the *Emma Dean* was let down another half mile to where the wreck of the *No Name* had been pushed into what today is called Lower Disaster Falls. Nearly split in half, it was wrapped against mid-river rocks. The loss was enormous. Two thousand pounds of equipment and food, the three men's personal gear, three rifles, a revolver, and Oramel's maps and notes thus far. Even worse, all of the irreplaceable barometers for measuring altitude had been mistakenly loaded into the one boat. The topographic surveying was now impossible.

Two men suggested taking the *Emma Dean* out to the wreck to try a salvage, but Powell stared at the wreck with gloomy eyes and forbade the attempt. Only after a sleepless night did he relent. Andy Hall, a 19-year-old immigrant from Scotland, challenged Sumner to join him. They rowed out with a few bumps to just below the mid-river rocks. Scrambling atop the wreck, one of them recovered some items, including old boots and the barometers! Powell watched in rapture as his men cheered the discovery, so pleased that they shared his enthusiasm for the science. But, as he looked closer, he realized the enthusiastic hollers were directed at a final item pulled from the hatch. A cask of whiskey that Howland had smuggled along—2 gallons according to Powell, or 10, according to Sumner. A volumetric historical discrepancy that remains unsolved to this day.

To return, it took Sumner and Hall a half hour of pushing and shimmying through boulders below the wreck. An omen. It would next take the expedition 10 total days to pass through the entire Canyon of Lodore—a distance of 12 miles, which is typically run in a day by modern river trips.

The 1869 adventure continues on page 95 . . .

3

LODORE, WHIRLPOOL, AND SPLIT MOUNTAIN CANYONS

THE STARTLING GEOLOGY AND IMPRESSIVE CANYONS of the Green River in Dinosaur National Monument offer perhaps the finest 4-day trip along the Powell route. Here, paddlers will encounter a sporty gradient, several challenging class III rapids, and Grand Canyon-esque scenery. Off the river, there are several worthy side hikes, many ancient petroglyphs to observe, and some great campsites—even if they're somewhat overmanicured by the NPS unit. Plus, near take-out, the must-see Quarry Exhibit Hall encloses a stone wall of 1,500 fossilized dinosaur bones. If you only have time for one short multiday trip from this book, this is it. (Vinyl record scratch.) But there's a problem. Obtaining a permit for a private river trip through Lodore requires winning the hardest lottery on the Powell route other than Grand Canyon.

In fact, if you want to go down Lodore privately (and you're reading this between midnight of December 1 and 11:59 p.m. of January 31), then, for the love of god, make 1 to 4 gallons of coffee and run, don't walk, to your nearest internet portal and begin your application. I'll wait . . . (Many moons pass.) Okay, you're back! You look pretty dazed. It's complicated stuff for just a 4-day trip, huh? But please know that despite the "dinosaurian"—bad pun,

A reproduction from a series of paintings by Rudolph Wendelin, commemorating the 1869 Powell expedition, is on display at the Powell Museum in Page, AZ.

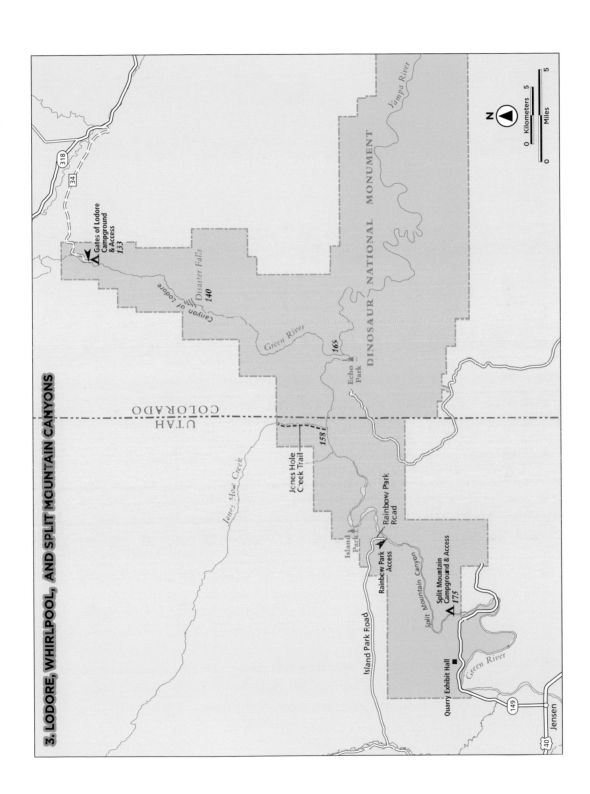

3. LODORE, WHIRLPOOL, AND SPLIT MOUNTAIN CANYONS

318

34

Gates of Lodore
Campground
& Access
133

Disaster Falls
140

Canyon of Lodore

Green River

165

Echo
Park

DINOSAUR NATIONAL MONUMENT

Yampa River

UTAH
COLORADO

Jones Hole Creek

Jones Hole
Creek Trail

158

Island Park Road

Island Park

Rainbow Park
Access

Rainbow Park
Road

Split Mountain Canyon

Split Mountain
Campground & Access
175

Quarry Exhibit Hall

Green River

149

40

Jensen

N

0   Kilometers   5

0   Miles   5

The Gates of Lodore, supposedly named for a very repetitive poem by Robert Southey or maybe a novel by Mary Shelley, author of *Frankenstein*. Let's just say, things got a little dark for the expedition once inside.

apologies—permit process and "brontosaurian"—just can't help myself—23 pages of regulations, Lodore is well worth all the fuss. Especially for diehard Powell pilgrims.

Shortly below put-in, the protruding Gates of Lodore are right up there with the brilliant flickers of Flaming Gorge in the award category for *most striking canyon entrances in a paddling route, historically themed*. In Echo Park, a vast amphitheater of sandstone is formed from Weber sandstone, where Powell's men spent days conversating with the walls. Just floating for 3 miles around Steamboat Rock is worth the trip for some people. Nearby, the startling folds of the Mitten Park Fault challenge the kaleidoscope of tilted strata in Rainbow Park for favorite crustal deformations. Running the river offers an opportunity to navigate the same rapids that almost derailed Powell's first expedition, including Disaster Falls, where the *No Name* was destroyed in 1869. Jones Hole offers a variety of activities, including hiking to petroglyphs, cooling off under a waterfall, or fly-fishing the stocked Jones Hole Creek.

A note to through-pilgrims. Most experts suggest acquiring a Grand Canyon permit first and then turning your attentions toward Dino. But many shoulder-season through-trip aspirations have been "T-rexed"—okay, last pun, I promise—by the Dino lottery. If you're looking at a late-summer to fall start for a potential through-pilgrimage, it may be worth considering starting with a Dino permit. Then, if you don't win a winter launch in the Grand Canyon lottery, you can try to obtain a cancellation permit through the follow-up lotteries. Risky, yes, but either method is a challenge.

Duration: 44 miles; most trips take 4 days, which is the max length allowed during high-use season; 5 days possible with special permission. During low-use season, max length is 6 days.

Access: Start at Gates of Lodore boat ramp (W40 43.64' / N108 53.30'). End at Split Mountain boat ramp (W40 26.73' / N109 15.16').

Logistics: Most trips hire a shuttle service to transport cars from Gates to Split. A self-shuttle, using CR 34, CR 10, CO 318, US 40, and UT 149, will take 2.5 hours one way.

Season and weather: The typical season is spring to fall; some have done Lodore in winter, when temps are often below freezing in the perpetual shade. Spring is mild to cool during the day, while summer months and early fall often reach the 90s. During

OUTFITTERS, SERVICES, AND SUPPLIES FOR DINO, UINTA BASIN, AND DESO

If you're traveling in from afar for runs in Segments 3, 4, or 5, there's a decent chance you'll pass through the Uinta Basin, where plenty of supplies are available. If your route comes in via backroads, consider stocking up farther afield.

River Runners Transport, in Vernal, UT, is an excellent full-service private outfitter, rental/equipment shop, and shuttle service; (800) 930-7238; www .riverrunnerstransport.com.

Wilkins River Car Shuttles; (435) 789-0507; www.wilkinsbuslines.com.

Redtail Air Adventures offers airplane shuttles for Deso/Gray; (435) 259-7421; flyredtail.com.

Supplies: The biggest full-service city is Vernal, UT. Craig, CO, and Rangely, CO, have some restaurants and stores. Jensen, UT, and Maybell, CO, have gas stations and convenience stores. Roosevelt has a few grocery stores and restaurants. Fort Duchesne has a grocery store. Myton has gas stations and convenience shops.

When Powell and crew called it Split Mountain, they really weren't kidding. Wedge yourself in there with a Lodore trip!

most of the year, snow is rare at river level, but thunderstorms are common. Elevation is 5,400' at the Gates and 4,800' at Split Mountain.

Water level and character: Flows above the confluence with the Yampa River primarily reflect releases from Flaming Gorge dam, found in the previous chapter. As the largest unregulated river remaining in the Colorado River basin, the Yampa significantly raises flows on the Green River in Echo Park. For levels below the confluence,

use USGS gauge Green River near Jensen, UT. At most water levels, this segment is class III, with Hell's Half Mile being III+ to IV; at higher flows, above 4,000–5,000 cfs, the river becomes class IV. Gradient is 13 fpm.

Challenges and safety: There's a decent number of midchannel rocks in the rapids, creating pin or wrap hazards. Make sure to scout the major rapids and bring a pin kit. Mosquitoes are a real challenge, especially at the Gates campground/boat ramp

One of the most iconic pictographs on the entire Powell route, this can be found at Jones Hole.

and Island Park, particularly when flows drop and leave stagnant pools. But, frankly, one of the biggest challenges is just keeping up with all the rules—for example, Dino requires 3 times the amount of spare life jackets than does the Grand Canyon, which is for a trip that's 5 times longer. Bring aspirin.

Boats: You can get down this segment with pretty much any type of whitewater boat, including hard-shell kayak, ducky, raft, dory, whitewater canoe. But watercraft with less than three air chambers, including SUPs, river boards, pack-rafts, and Shredders or paddlecats, are only allowed with support craft, like rafts or dories.

Camping: Sites are assigned by the river office; boaters can list their preferences on their permit application.

Agencies, regulations, fees: So you say you like long and complex lists of rules, do you? Well, does Dinosaur National Monument have a gift for you with their 23-page booklet *Boating in the Monument: Information & Regulations*, which is available for download from their website and must be reviewed by all boaters. Next up, the fees. (Alternating drum rolls followed by the melody to REM's "It's the End of the World.") There are application fees, entrance fees, campground fees, permit fees, multiday fees, 1-day fees, overlength fees, penalty fees. That's the end of the fees . . . as I know it; (970) 374-2468; www.nps.gov/dino.

Lottery and permit: Lottery applications for high-use season are accepted on recreation.gov between Dec 1 and Jan 31 for trips later that year. High-use season is typically mid-May to mid-Sept (see website for exact dates each season), with the rest of the year considered low-use season. Winners are notified around mid-Feb and have 2 weeks to claim their permits, complete their reservation, and pay remaining fees. Beginning Mar 1, 2018, low-use season permits, unclaimed high-use season permits, and day permits are available by first-come basis on recreation.gov or through the call center at (877) 444-6777.

Maps: The two best options for topographic river maps are *Belknap's Waterproof Dinosaur River Guide* and *RiverMaps' Guide to the Green and Yampa Rivers in Dinosaur National Monument.*

Highlights: Well, just floating through the Gates, about 133 miles down the route, to start. • Winnie's Rapid really announces itself, you'll see. • Upper and Lower Disaster Falls are great rapids, and that much better given the history of 1869. • Triplet Fall and Hell's Half Mile have real character. • The Rippling Brook viewpoint is well worth the short hike. • About 17 river miles from the Gates, Mitten Park fault is like a geologic finger trap game. • About 152 miles down the route, Echo Park. I feel like I talk about this one a lot, almost as if there's a—what's the word? Where something keeps repeating. • The backside of Mitten is even more twisted. • Not far into Whirlpool Canyon is the test site for proposed but defeated Echo Park dam. • Jones Hole Creek offers great creekside hike, waterfalls, pictographs, fly fishing. • Island Park, 163 paddling miles from Green River (Station), like you're traveling back in time. • Rainbow Park— oh, wait, more rapids, too. • Don't just drive away from the exit to Split Mountain, about 175 miles down the Powell route, but check out the various viewpoints to get a visual handle on what's going on.

Commercial outfitters: (private outfitters, shuttles, and supplies on page 65)

Adrift Adventures offers commercial raft trips, including 4-day Lodore, 1-day Split Mountain, 5-day Yampa; (800) 824-0150; adrift.com.

Adventure Bound USA offers commercial raft trips, including 3- or 4-day Lodore, 4- or 5-day Yampa; (800) 423-4668; adventureboundusa.com.

ARTA offers commercial raft trips, including 4-day Lodore, 5-day Yampa; (800) 323-2782; www.arta.org.

Dinosaur River Expeditions offers commercial raft trips, including 4-day Lodore, 4- or 5-day Yampa; (800) 345-7238; www.dinosaurriverexpeditions.com.

Eagle Outdoor Sports offers commercial raft trips, including 4-day Lodore, 5-day Yampa; (801) 382-7238; rafteagle.com.

LONG DAYS IN LODORE; OR, WHAT'S THE DEAL WITH DINO?

At the boat ramp near Gates of Lodore, the ranger was inspecting our required equipment. River toilet? Check. Buckets? Check. First-aid kit, safety rope, kitchen strainer? Check, check, check. Our eight-person crew—four in kayaks, four in two rafts—milled about, trying to act casual. The mood was only slightly reminiscent of a boot camp film. When the ranger made a disappointed face during PFD review, I was perfectly willing to drop and give him twenty pushups if deemed appropriate.

"I'm going to have to disqualify two of these spare life jackets," he said, pointing out one that had a decorative patch sewn into the nylon material—affixed by the manufacturer but still an issue. After all, how could the ranger know that the manufacturer—despite being one of the top PFD makers in America—didn't puncture the flotation foam when installing the patch? The other PFD was technically the right coast guard type, but it was clearly designed for water skiing and not whitewater. Why it couldn't serve as an emergency backup—should a total of four life jackets mysteriously vanish during our 4-day trip—was not addressed. (*Notes to self*: Possible life jacket thieves downstream. Also, why *doesn't* anyone water ski through whitewater?)

The ranger was perfectly friendly about the situation, and we didn't hold the rules against him at all. He explained there was a solution, so we could still go on our early-July trip through Dinosaur National Monument. The park service would loan us, free of charge, an additional two PFDs for the trip. A half hour later, with our full complement of three spare lifejackets safely onboard a third raft brought in just to haul required extra equipment, we floated toward the iconic Gates of Lodore.

Finally, we were off! On our fourth fresh-eyes descent on the Powell route—meaning none of us had ever boated these canyons before. The approach gave each trip an exciting exploratory feel but often meant some extra headaches when navigating the complex—not going to say nitpicky, oh crap, I just did—regulations of an infamous bureaucracy like Dino.

Over the course of the project, I'd been warned many times that Dino was "special." To be honest, most people were much harsher, describing the management practitioners as a body part often compared to opinions that all people have. Learning this over the years, I'd originally chalked it up to regulation resentment. But hear enough stories, I start to wonder. Experience it myself, I start to understand.

At Green River Lakes, a boater told the story of a Dino private trip involving an evening campsite skinny dip. Oh, the horror. By chance, an on-river ranger floated past. At take-out a day later, a ranger was waiting to write a pricey ticket for indecent exposure. One member of the private trip happened to be Dutch. After

Hell's Half Mile is a class III+ rapid found 12 miles into Lodore Canyon.

hearing the accent, the ranger hesitated. Were these free spirited Europeans? Or just regular old birthday-suit Americans? My new friend, knowing just a bit of Dutch himself, began jabbering random vocabulary phrases, like *red boat, tall man,* and *no pants*, so they dodged a ticket and snagged a story.

Other complaints are too numerous to list. Many focus on the lottery system, which has admittedly improved in recent years. Some boaters have failed for decades to win a high-season Dino permit while the Grand Canyon went to a weighted lottery to address this very issue. Others point to the exhaustive list of regulations for a 4-day trip. Many of these, including leave-no-trace practices, are perfectly reasonable. But other rules are more stringent than a 3-week Grand Canyon trip.

I've even met rangers, working on other parts of the Powell route, who complain about the management in Dino. One such ranger is unofficially boycotting this favorite section, yet still offered a compassionate appraisal of the situation. "Look," he told me, "when you're a river ranger, it takes a lot of effort to not become a total a-hole." He explained that some visitors display questionable behavior on the managed rivers. It can make the job pretty tough, and some

Rippling Brook viewpoint is one of those iconic vistas found along the Powell route, about 1 mile down from Hell's Half Mile.

rangers respond by moving toward authoritarianism. That seems understandable but not necessarily excusable. Especially when the concerns are nearly universal among rank-and-file boaters.

I wish I could report we aced our Dino exam on our 4-day fresh-eyes trip. But, sadly, it was only 6 hours before we made—before I made, as the trip leader—a

key mistake. After a fun descent through splashy class III rapids between the sheer walls of Lodore, we approached our assigned camp at Pot Creek. Suddenly, I realized I'd stowed the permit that listed our exact campsite number.

"Does anyone remember if we're in Pot Creek 1 or 2?" I called out. We'd glanced the night before while organizing gear, but in the flurry of rigging and inspection that morning, I'd completely forgotten to double-check.

"Pretty sure it's number 2," said one friend, while another replied, "That sounds right."

In hindsight, I should have just asked everyone to stop in an eddy above Pot Creek, but we were tired. We'd all driven in from the east the day before, and we were itching for a break. We floated right past #1 to #2 and built our camp. An hour later, a massive commercial trip arrived. I grabbed the permit, saw the error, and ran out to apologize. Fully embarrassed, I offered that we'd move our camp by foot and give up the sandy beach. The first commercial guide, about my age, was understandably annoyed. But he countered that his trip might be willing to move to Kolb campsite, a mile downstream.

Then, a second raft came in hot, with an older guide about twice our age already shouting. He tossed his bowline at my buddy and was in my face in an instant. Suddenly I was back in cinematic boot camp again. I'd messed everything up, he said, using far more colorful language. He didn't care if I was sorry. I needed to fix the disaster I'd caused. I needed to get our boats off their beach. Where to wasn't his problem. My buddy made a joke he might just let go of the angry raft guide's bow line. The older guide said we'd have to push our two rafts up the river. I looked and saw a minor rapid in between. The guests in the older guide's raft looked stricken with confusion. Now I was getting upset, so I walked up a trail between camps to see if it was possible to safely wade or line the rafts upstream.

While I was gone, tensions reportedly eased. A compromise was reached. Once he calmed down, the older raft guide's concern was relayed. A third trip may have been assigned to Kolb camp, and the situation might worsen later that day. None of us knew how many groups launched on the river that day. So, it was agreed that we'd station someone above Pot Creek 1 to wave in any group that arrived.

In the Quarry Exhibit Hall, which you can access at the Dino NM visitor center, you can view fossilized dinosaur bones preserved as they were discovered in a cliff face, including these femur bones from an apatosaurus (top) and diplodocus (bottom). There will be a quiz later on.

And that's what I did. For 4 hours, I accepted my penance and waited above Pot Creek until dark and I was certain no group was coming.

The next day, we floated past the commercial group, and I apologized again. We'd never been to Dino—nor any river with assigned sites. We'd be more careful the next time. All was forgiven with friendly waves and smiles, so we floated onward to an amazing 3 days. The mishap was entirely my fault. I should have been more careful when reviewing the permit. But a few friends did wonder why we'd spent over an hour during our launch inspection dealing with spare life jackets, without so much as a reminder of the campsite situation. And speaking of next times, it didn't seem like most of them were excited to come back.

At take-out, before we'd even secured our boats, a ramp attendant came asking for our permit. When the commercial group arrived a short time later and was asked the same thing before touching land, the older guide nearly went full boot camp again. *Run for your life*, I thought. While we put away gear, three rangers arrived. One approached for a post-trip inspection.

"You look nervous," she boasted.

"You don't know the difference between annoyance and nervousness," said my buddy under his breath.

Before we could start, a stiff wind struck the ramp, which soon picked up into a sand-strewn microburst. In an instant, our unloaded raft was violently barrel-rolled across the river surface a hundred yards upstream. Paddles and dry bags flung across the ramp onto nearby boulders. One friend ducked behind my truck, nearly impaled by a flying oar. I'd never seen anything like it. Never seen a group of rangers laugh harder in my life, either.

While I swam into the river to retrieve the boat, I heard the rangers joking about how common these winds are. Upon returning, I considered inviting them to a hilarious hilltop I know that's frequented by lightning. But instead we just packed up after a final long day in Lodore.

I don't imagine most of our crew will ever go back, though I hope to myself. And I don't imagine too many of them would raise much of a fuss if the corporate-industrial complex ever comes knocking at Dino's door, talking about shrinking the monument with designs on short-term exploitation. And that's a shame because Dino protects about 100 miles, on the Green and Yampa Rivers, of the most unique canyons in the United States. Plus, with all the cultural artifacts and historic sites, it more than satisfies the Antiquities Act.

But at some point, if nearly every river runner shares the same concerns, it seems reasonable to ask, *What's the deal with Dino?* Certainly, the problem is not the very concept of regulation, but perhaps the application? Due to entrenched bureaucracy? Poor training and leadership? Do they just need a hug? When stewards behave more like security guards, it's easy to wonder if Dino's practices aren't fencing out the same stake-holders that would fight for its preservation, should the unfortunate time ever come. And recreational paddlers are pretty good huggers, at least when they're not wearing four life jackets.

Winnie's Rock, the first midchannel obstacle in the Canyon of Lodore, is not just for wrapping rafts. Get your boof on with NOLS kayaking instructor Justin Kleberg!
KIRK RASMUSSEN/NOLS

Holiday Expeditions offers commercial raft trips, including 4-day Lodore, 4- or 5-day Yampa; (800) 624-6323; www.bikeraft.com.

OARS offers commercial raft trips, including 3- to 5-day Lodore, 1-day Split Mountain, 4- to 5-day Yampa; (800) 346-6277; www.oars.com.

Sherri Griffith Expeditions offers commercial raft trips, including 4-day Lodore and 4- to 5-day Yampa; (800) 332-2439; www.griffithexp.com.

National Outdoor Leadership School (NOLS) offers various paddling and rowing courses that include trips through Dino; www.nols.edu.

PADDLING: SPLIT MOUNTAIN DAILY

On the Green River from Rainbow Park to Split Mountain, this is the only day trip within the canyons portion of Dino. The section is mostly class II–III, with a 20 fpm gradient, good current, and frequent rapids. All details from the larger segment apply, except for those below.

Duration: 8 miles, ½ day

Access: Start at Rainbow Park boat ramp (W40 29.70' / N109 10.42'). End at Split Mountain boat ramp (W40 26.73' / N109 15.16').

Imagined conversation in 1869: "Let's see, we already used Flaming and Red—I'm thinking Tangerine or, curveball, Spark Canyon? Anyone got anything?" Rainbow Park, 169 paddling miles down the route.

This book very well could have been titled *Stuff to Do Above and Below Echo Park.* And some suits wanted to dam this? Dam this?! Damn that.

Logistics: Shuttles can be arranged through either River Runners or Wilkins, listed above. A self-shuttle, using UT 149, Brush Creek Rd., Island Park Rd., and Rainbow Park Rd., takes 28 miles and about 1 hour each way.

Lottery and permit: There's no lottery, but daily permits must be applied for in advance using the reservation system at recreation.gov under Dinosaur National Monument—Split Mountain Permits, UT.

Camping: No camping is allowed for anyone on the 8 miles of Split Mountain Daily. There is a small, primitive campground at Rainbow Park and a larger campground at Split Mountain.

Heck yeah, Weber sandstone makes an appearance on the Yampa. It's all over this place.
AMY MARTIN

OTHER PADDLING: YAMPA RIVER

This is the other classic multiday river trip available in Dinosaur National Monument. The Yampa is undammed, so this trip is only possible when natural flows are suitable, from snow melt during spring and early summer. The trip typically begins at Deerlodge Park and ends at Split Mountain on the Green River. The total trip is 71 river miles, with about 46 miles on the Yampa. The Yampa joins the Green River in Echo Park and continues 25 miles to the usual Split Mountain take-out. A few of the many highlights are the famous Tiger Wall and an extra-long traverse of the same rocks that compose Echo Park—I'm kind of a Weber sandstone guy, so I definitely approve. Find more info on the Dino website.

4

UINTA BASIN

BELOW SPLIT MOUNTAIN, THE GREEN RIVER EMERGES from tortured folds of Weber sandstone into a wide valley of low bluffs and farmed floodplains. For many Powell route paddlers, the Green through Uinta Basin seems a forgotten river. Perhaps noticed briefly from the US 40 bridge near Jensen, just outside Dinosaur National Monument, but likely dismissed as boring and flat. But for 100 miles, the river meanders through pleasant curves, around midchannel sandbars, and between cottonwood groves until the stark cliffs of upper Desolation begin to rise. In the basin, you'll need to try to not spot antelope and other riparian wildlife.

While improved access points are limited throughout the basin, several options for flatwater paddling exist, from a day trip below Split Mountain or through Ouray National Wildlife Refuge, to a pair of 3- or 4-day trips above and below Ouray NWR, to a weeklong trip through the entire basin. Paddlers with Desolation/Gray permits occasionally begin their trips in the basin to float through the gradual beginnings of Desolation Canyon, about 20 river miles above Sand Wash.

This segment includes plenty of the modern contradictions common along the Powell route of today. Despite passing through a fairly populated valley—at least by rural Utah standards—the river is removed from most development and offers one of the more remote experiences in this book. And while this segment offers plenty of solitude, it is certainly not of the pristine variety found in the managed wilderness areas elsewhere along the route.

Here, the river regularly passes oil derricks, pipelines, irrigation diversions, and center-spigot farm fields. But with these industrial elements mostly removed, at short or long distances, from water level, the result is limited intrusiveness—in fact, they add a surreal quality. To me, the Green River through Uinta Basin feels like a pseudo-rural-industrial-wilderness of the type often dramatized in postapocalyptic movies. As if there were once many people from various cultures and periods present. But they vanished, leaving behind still-running machinery and intact artifacts that speak to a

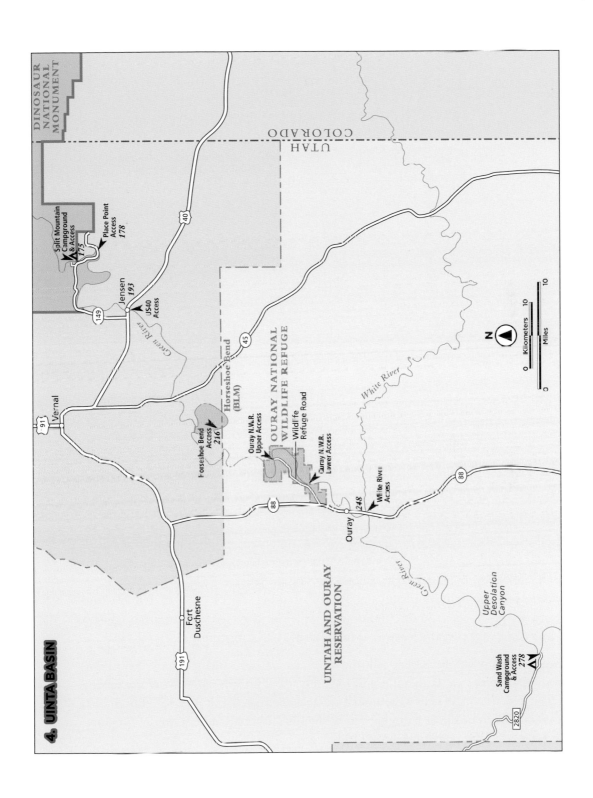

September thunderstorms drift past Horseshoe Bend (yes, another one!) in the Uinta Basin.

different time. Somewhat like what happened to the Fremont culture that once populated the canyons of the following segment.

Duration: 103 miles; 6–9 days.

Access: Through-segment paddlers should start at Split Mountain boat ramp (W40 26.73' / N109 15.16') in Dinosaur National Monument. End at Sand Wash launch area (W39 50.42' / N109 54.83').

Logistics: Private vehicles can be safely parked, long-term, at Split Mountain and Sand Wash; none of the other access points in this segment seem suitable for safe long-term parking. No overnight parking is allowed in Ouray National Wildlife Reserve. A self-shuttle between Split Mountain and Sand Wash using UT 149, US 40, US 191, and Sand Wash Rd. takes almost 3 hours each way. Shuttle services can be arranged with River Runners Transport for trips of most lengths and using most access locations.

Season and weather: Spring–fall; the river can ice over during winter. Midspring to midfall temps are fairly mild, but lows can still dip to freezing. We're not talking about a lot of rainfall here—the annual average in Vernal, UT, is under 9"! But sudden thunderstorms or showers can happen at any time during paddling season. Elevation at Ouray, UT, is approximately 4,700'.

Water level and character: Class I, with an occasional class I+ to II riffle—yeah, that's a thing—mostly during higher spring flows. Gradient is about 2 fpm. For water levels use guage USGS Green River near Jensen, UT.

Challenges and safety: Other than the shuttle sitch, mosquitoes are probably the biggest challenge. There are many stagnant pools for them to propagate. They can be especially thick when high spring flows recede. There have been cases of White Nile virus, from mosquitoes, reported in the basin. Come prepared. There is little shade in this segment, so be wary of sun exposure.

Boats: Really anything for flatwater; touring or sea kayak, canoe, SUP, even raft, which may be slow moving at lower water levels.

Camping: This is tricky in the Uinta Basin. To start, no camping is allowed in Ouray NWR or Stewart Lake Waterfowl Management Area. Next, much of the land along the Green River is either private property or tribal lands that are part of the Uintah and Ouray Reservation, where camping is not allowed without permission. There are also extensive holdings of Utah School Trust Lands, which were set up to fund state public education through resource extraction, land leasing, and sales. Plus, there are sporadic holdings of the Bureau of Land Management. While BLM land or nonleased trust land is open to camping, specific land status is rarely marked from river level. One option is to obtain a detailed land status map from publiclands.org or trustlands

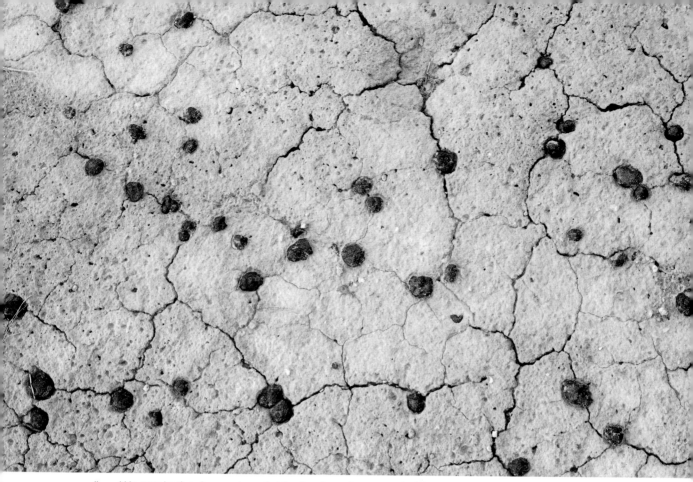

" . . . We saw in the depressions flat beds of sand, surrounded by hundreds of small round balls of stone an inch or so in diameter, like marbles . . .," wrote Frederick Dellenbaugh, crew member and artist on the second expedition. Today these concretions are called *moqui marbles* and are commonly associated with Navajo sandstone.

.utah.gov/resources/maps/gis-data-and-maps/county-maps. Another option is to go when flows are lower, and camp on the plentiful sandbars and midchannel islands.

Agencies, regulations, fees: The land bordering the river may be BLM, Utah School Trust Lands, Uinta and Ouray Reservations lands, or private.

Maps: The best river maps for this segment are found in *Belknap's Waterproof Desolation River Guide.*

Highlights: Floating through the foothills below Split Mountain. • About 210 miles down the Powell route, the Green River has its own 8-mile Horseshoe Bend. • Ouray National Wildlife Refuge starts about 57 miles from Split Mountain. • The White River enters about 247 miles down the route. • Upper Desolation Canyon begins about 12 miles from Ouray, which makes for a great extension to a Deso trip.

PADDLING: DAY TRIPS FROM SPLIT MOUNTAIN

If you're in the area to visit Dinosaur National Monument or run an upstream section, and you want to keep the watery fun going, why not paddle out through the diminishing but scenic foothills below Split Mountain that give way to the open country of Uinta Basin. The nearby Quarry Exhibit Hall is definitely worth a stop, and there are some excellent short hikes in this part of the monument.

Duration: 3.25 or 17.5 miles; 1–2 hours or 1 long day

Access: Start at Split Mountain boat ramp (W40 26.73' / N109 15.16'). Small craft only, no rafts, may use Place Point access (W40 24.39' / N109 14.30') or US 40 Bridge/Jensen access (W40.21.94' / N109 19.99').

Logistics: Self-shuttle from Split Mountain to Place Point is less than 10 minutes on UT 49 and entirely inside the monument. From Split to Jensen access, using UT 49 and US 40, is 10 miles and 20 minutes. Note that the access on Jensen, river-left just downstream from the US 40 bridge, is an unofficial access that has been used by small numbers of river runners for years, but it may be considered private property.

Agencies, regulations, fees: There is an entry fee for Dinosaur National Monument (NPS) and a ton of regulations; visit the monument website or see Segment 3 for more info.

PADDLING: SPLIT MOUNTAIN TO OURAY

Since there aren't any public long-term parking options in or around Ouray and the wildlife refuge, you'll need a shuttle pick-up to run this section. A highlight is circling around Horseshoe Bend—that's right, Utah has its own Horseshoe Bend. No, it's not quite as impressive as Arizona's, but it's still cool, and almost no one knows about it. Camping is tricky here (see segment details above).

Duration: 40–72.5 miles, with intermediate lengths possible; 2–6 days

Access: Take your pick! Split Mountain, Jensen (coordinates above), Horseshoe Bend (N40 15.80' / W109 32.21'), Ouray NRW upper access, lower access, or White River access (coordinates below).

Logistics: River Runner Transport can help you. Driving time between Split and Ouray is about 1 hour one way, if you can find a friend to help you.

Agencies, regulations, fees: If you put in at Split, there's an entrance fee to Dino NM. Otherwise, there are many agencies to contend with. Camping on tribal land may be possible with specific permission and permit/fee. Contact and info for the Uintah and Ouray Indian Tribe can be found at www.utetribe.com.

Below Split Mountain, the Green River winds through decreasing cliffs of Dinosaur National Monument and into the Uinta Basin.

PADDLING: OURAY NATIONAL WILDLIFE REFUGE

This day trip is a bit out of the way from, well, everywhere in the universe. Which might be the perfect reason to do it. There's no camping in the refuge, while outside there are pockets of public land that show clear signs of overnight visitation—but identifying them can be tricky. If you're on the way to other points (relatively) nearby, like Sand Wash or Dino, this could be a fine spot to do a quick half-day flatwater float.

Duration: 6.5, 9, or 15.5 miles; 2-3 hours up to all day

Reeds! Hey, please don't put the book down! Am I the only one who gets all hot and bothered by reeds? These particular reeds can be found in Ouray National Wildlife Refuge.

Access: In Ouray NWR, there are two gravel/dirt ramps, an upper access (N40 10.94' / W109 35.75') and 6.5 river miles downstream, a lower access (N40 8.67' / W109 37.76'). Nine river miles downstream from the lower access in the refuge, there's a gravel access on the White River (N40 3.85' / W109 40.37'), just upstream from its confluence with Green River.

Logistics: A self-shuttle between the upper and lower access points in the refuge, using the interior Wildlife Refuge Rd. and a connector road, is 5 miles and 10 minutes one way. From the lower access to White River access, using Wildlife Refuge Rd., UT 88/Seep Ridge Rd., and White River Access Road, it's about 15 minutes and 7 miles each way.

Agencies, regulations, fees: There are no fees to enter Ouray National Wildlife Refuge, but you can't park overnight. (435) 545-2522; www.fws.gov/refuge/ouray.

PADDLING: OURAY TO SAND WASH

You'll need a shuttle service dropoff or a very generous friend to run this section. There is no public long-term parking in Ouray. The highlight with this section is

Multiday kayakers enjoy lunch on a sandbar, complete with sun umbrellas. Not far downstream, the river enters Desolation Canyon. Dumm, dumm, dumm. . . .

Jonathan Bowler is a full-time river advocate who has boated every stretch of the Powell route and spent thousands of nights on the shores of the Green and Colorado Rivers. He's a founder of the river-advocacy nonprofit Rig to Flip, and his University of Wyoming master's thesis assessed recreation opportunities in the Uinta Basin. He lives in Condon, MT, where he is academic director at Swan Valley Connections and teaches public land policy, watershed dynamics, and native fish ecology for college field programs.

Mike: What first attracted you to visit and study the Uinta Basin?

Jonathan: Belknap's river guide for Desolation has a photograph of the Green River in the Uinta Basin with a raft, rigged to perfection, tied to shore at Tia Juana Bottom. That one photograph was the single most influential attraction [to visit]. But the old Belknap guide used to start the description for the southern Uinta Basin with the sentence "A popular starting point for trips through Desolation Canyon. . . ." In later editions, this first sentence was taken out—an omission that told me at some point boaters stopped beginning [Deso] trips in the Uinta Basin. That led me to conduct my master's research on river management and river users' choices for recreation.

Much of the Uinta Basin has a mysterious quality, like everyone vanished but forgot their flip-flops.

Mike: Why do you keep going back?

Jonathan: When I first boated through the basin, we stopped and took that same photo [like Belknap's] of our boats tied to shore at Tia Juana Bottom. It was a rite of passage, similar to arriving at Lees Ferry for a Grand Canyon float, except in the Uinta Basin, it's a much more intimate feel, like you are traveling on a forgotten river. The sunsets seem to last for days [due to] the lack of sheer canyon walls. Birdsong fills side channels as you round the many vegetated islands. Whitetail deer, elk, moose, wild mustangs—it's truly an oasis where you can escape the crowds and experience true solitude. I have boated through five separate times—the Uinta Basin is a figurative blank spot on the river recreationist's map.

A group of touring kayakers on a multiday trip caravan down the Green River through the Uinta Basin, proving, yes, people do paddle here!

Mike: What did you learn from your study?

Jonathan: I wanted to understand why the basin has less than 100 boaters each year when Dinosaur National Monument's river permits [upstream] are used to capacity at over 10,000 users per year and Desolation Canyon's [downstream] at over 4,000 users per year. To investigate, I posted myself at Split Mountain Boat Ramp and Sand Wash for two summers and distributed surveys to river runners. The surveys asked why they chose their recreation setting, their reasons for the activity, and what benefits they received. It turned out that most users did not focus on setting but on benefits such as group camaraderie, escape from pressures of daily life, a feeling of solitude, and being in nature. Whitewater, adventure, and thrill seeking were some of the lowest rated responses. My team and I found that the Uinta Basin can very well produce these same benefits and perhaps with greater effect when discussing solitude, wildlife, and engagement with nature.

Mike: Like many boaters, I know you're fascinated by Powell. How did he feel about the basin?

Jonathan: Powell and his men called it Antelope Valley, after the Indian name *Won'sits Yu-av*. The Uinta Basin provided the expedition an opportunity to observe latitude and longitude, to travel to the Uinta Indian Reservation Agency for resupply, and to catalog ethnographic information from the region's native populations.

Powell describes the river with appeal: "Now our way is along a gently flowing river, beset with many islands; groves are seen on either side, and natural meadows, where herds of antelope are feeding." Later, as they neared Desolation Canyon [he wrote], "We find quiet water today, the river sweeping in great and beautiful curves, the cañon walls steadily increasing in altitude." After coming from the toil and hardship of the Canyon of Lodore and Split Mountain, Antelope Valley must have been a wonderful respite!

floating through the beginnings of upper Desolation Canyon. This would make a good upstream addition to a Deso/Gray trip.

Duration: 46, 39.5, or 30.5 miles; 2–4 days

Access: Start at upper or lower access points in Ouray NWR or the White River access. Stop at Sand Wash access. (All coordinates above.)

Logistics: Ouray to Sand Wash is 2.25 hours one way, but maybe don't tell your friends that until they pick you up?

A pair of antelope graze above the confluence of the White and Green Rivers, about 250 paddling miles down the route.

Agencies, regulations, fees: There are pockets of BLM land and tribal land within the Uintah and Ouray Indian Reservation. The Ute tribe's camping permit for Desolation Canyon should apply for the river-left/eastern bank below roughly mile 82, where the canyon walls begin to rise. See segment 5 for information about Sand Wash (BLM).

OTHER PADDLING: WHITE RIVER

A tributary of the Green below Ouray, this is a popular float stream during spring runoff but is typically too low during other times of year. A popular section is between Bonanza and Enron. To explore this tributary, your best approach may be to arrange a shuttle from River Runners or Wilkins.

1869, PART III: INTO DESOLATION WITH THE JUDGMENT AND LUCK OF SCHOOLBOYS

Goodbye, eyebrows; hello, Echo Park • 1869 origins of the whitewater snob • let's steal a stew! • climbing with underwear, swimming with bedrolls

On June 16, the 8th day in the Canyon of Lodore and the 24th day of the expedition, Bradley made an observation. The harder rocks that form cliffs and rapids in the Canyon of Lodore—much of it reddish quartzites today called the Uinta Mountain Group—were subsiding, and an overlying layer of softer rock, the whitish Weber sandstone, was approaching river level. The men rightfully hoped the intense whitewater would soon cease.

But before Lodore would let them go, 2 more days of toil ensued, including a boat squirting across the river during a lining. Next, a wind-fanned fire ignited their camp. In an instant, the brush was ablaze from cliffs to river. Men hastily snatched up some burning clothes but lost others that had been spread to dry. Half afire themselves, one man snatched a burning handkerchief from his neck, while another had a hole burned into his long underwear. They rushed to the boats, dropping down through a minor rapid. In the chaos, the crew's mess kit was lost overboard.

Downstream, they laughed for an hour at the ridiculous situation. Henceforth, Oramel joked that Hawkins would have to stir beans with pickax and shovel, while the men drank coffee from bailing pails. Also lost were Bradley's eyebrows. A development that reinforced a journal comment he made 2 days before that if the expedition succeeded, it would not be due to good judgment but dumb luck. And the men, particularly demonstrated by their many unsuccessful hunts, were more like schoolboys on holiday than men accustomed to living by the chase.

On June 18, 10 days after entering Lodore, the expedition passed the Yampa River and entered Echo Park. They spent 2 days in this wonderful amphitheater, counting

Echo Park, where the Yampa joins the Green River, in 1871; J. K. Hillers. US GEOLOGICAL SURVEY

the echoes of their voices off Steamboat Rock. The fish were so big—a yard long—that Bradley lost four hooks and three lines to them before twining four lines together. Soon, the men landed a few 10- to 15-pounders.

The Yampa doubled the flow of the Green River. Below, the channel was wider with less exposed boulders. In Whirlpool and Split Mountain Canyons, more rapids and wave trains appeared. Some were lined, while others were run—including one rapid stern first, an accident by a freight boat. After missing an eddy, it dragged 120 feet of uncoiled bowline down the rapid. Oramel later remarked, "When we have to run the rapids, nothing is more exhilarating; it keeps in play a rapid train of thought and action. . . . After having run the fall, one feels like hurrahing. . . . A calm smooth

Lighthouse Rock roughly marks the division between upper and lower Deso. As it appeared to E. O. Beaman in 1871. US GEOLOGICAL SURVEY

The iconic Gunnison Butte at the end of Gray Canyon in 1871; J. K. Hillers. US GEOLOGICAL SURVEY

stream, running only at the rate of five or six miles per hour, is a horror we all detest now." Or, as some modern whitewater-or-nothing enthusiasts comment, "Flatwater, ugh." On June 26, the expedition spilled out from the cracked shell of Split Mountain and into the Uinta Basin to a hundred miles of "horror"—or as some river explorers comment, "More paddling, yes!"

Despite the sluggish current, as the men rowed, they enjoyed the vast beauty of the valley. They birdwatched and hunted geese in lands that later became a wildlife refuge. They passed local Native Americans' vegetable gardens and bottom croplands of corn, wheat, and potato. Instead of grueling portages every 0.5 mile, the new fights were with clouds of mosquitoes. At the mouth of the Uinta River, today called the Duchesne River, they made a basecamp amid stands of cottonwood. Here, Frank Goodman announced he was leaving the expedition, in part due to the loss of his personal gear after the experience at Disaster Falls. He joined Powell and three others in walking the "short" 25 miles to the Uinta Agency, a US government outpost that managed the valley's reservation.

While at the agency, Powell sent letters from himself and the men to various parties, including newspapers. This would be welcome news, as several inaccurate accounts were circulating the country. There was even a hoaxster fictitiously describing a scene where Powell and 20 men disappeared into a whirlpool in a way suspiciously similar to Ahab and the *Pequod* in *Moby-Dick*. On the return, Powell brought two Ute tribesmen, the first encountered, who would carry back to the agency some items Powell had traded to obtain a 300-pound sack of flour, a resupply selection that some of the men, restless from the long layover, would come to later grumble about.

After 10 days, on July 6, the group of nine continued downstream. Just below the White River, the men stopped on an island. There was a vegetable garden they'd been invited to "steal" from, supposedly planted by a white hunter and trader with a Native American wife. Grabbing beets, carrots, turnips, and potatoes, the men skipped town despite the invite. They floated down to a cottonwood island for lunch, cooking all of the vegetables in a stew, including the potato tops as greens. Bradley thought they tasted so bad, he threw them all away. But the others chowed down and were soon vomiting freely.

The next day, on the river, the walls of what was named Desolation Canyon began to slowly rise, and the men periodically stopped to measure altitude or explore. Bradley and Powell climbed a mountain. Reaching a sheer precipice, they scrambled from ledge to ledge, until Powell found himself clutching an outcrop with his only hand, unable to proceed farther. Now he was stuck, perched precariously high above the rocks. Thinking quickly, Bradley climbed above and lowered his drawers (or long underwear), creating one of the most comically dramatic moments from the expedition. While giving full credit to Bradley, Powell oddly misplaced the event as occurring on the Yampa, just one of many alterations Powell made in his 1875 account, which has puzzled historians ever since.

Progressing into the inner gorge of Deso, they came upon rapids, most of which they ran. "It is a wild and exciting game," wrote Bradley. If not for the danger of losing food or equipment and having to hike out to civilization, he wished they could run them all. Instead, Powell seemed to emerge from Lodore more cautious, and he called for portages that Bradley felt could be rowed. "Major's way is safe but I as a lazy man look more to the ease of the thing."

Attempting to run a rapid, the *Emma Dean* broke one oar and lost another. Seeing no timber from which to cut new oars, the pilot boat continued through the next drop, swamped, and rolled the men out. Powell, the only man equipped with a life jacket, swam for shore. Meanwhile, Sumner and Dunn swam the boat out of the river. In the process, they lost their bed rolls, two rifles, and a barometer, and ruined some watches. Onshore, they searched for wood to build new oars. Shortly after, another upset saw Bradley flung from the boat. He caught his foot on the seat and was dragged through the water for a spell. Eventually, the men passed into Coal Canyon, later renamed Gray. Along the way, they ran more rapids than they lined, before exiting into another wide valley, where Gunnison Butte still rises from the Book Cliffs.

The 1869 adventure continues on page 136 . . .

DESOLATION AND GRAY CANYONS

NOWHERE ELSE ALONG THE POWELL ROUTE do two adjacent canyons have drearier names than this amazing 83-mile section that's anything but as it cuts a colorful gash through the Tavaputs Plateau. So far, we Powell pilgrims have come through flaming gorges and gates of Lodores and echo parks and split mountains. Yes, there were a few boring designations along the way—Browns Park is a great spot, but the label suggests a fertilizer-themed fairground. And, here, in our 5th segment, the Powell expedition marketing department really outdid themselves. You mean we can follow up desolation with a gray palette scheme? Hot damn! In fact, Sherri Griffith Expeditions

Just one of many picturesque campsites on a Deso trip.

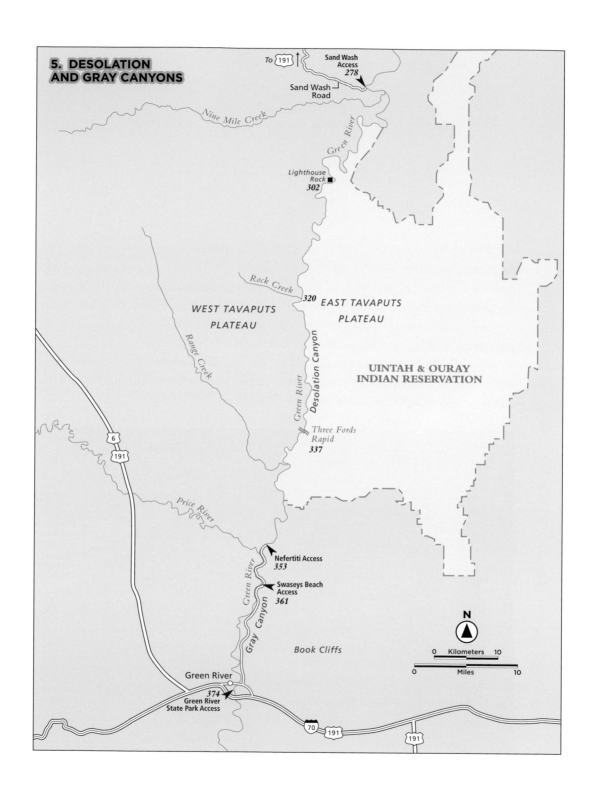

5. DESOLATION AND GRAY CANYONS

To 191

Sand Wash Access
278

Sand Wash Road

Nine Mile Creek

Green River

Lighthouse Rock
302

Rock Creek

320

WEST TAVAPUTS PLATEAU

EAST TAVAPUTS PLATEAU

Range Creek

Green River

Desolation Canyon

UINTAH & OURAY INDIAN RESERVATION

Three Fords Rapid
337

Price River

Nefertiti Access
353

Green River

Swaseys Beach Access
361

Gray Canyon

Book Cliffs

Green River

374
Green River State Park Access

N

0   Kilometers   10

0   Miles   10

A short hike across the Uintah and Ouray Indian Reservation (permit required) into Firewater Canyon leads to a moonshiner's cabin.

in some descriptions calls this trip Majestic Canyons, while the out-of-print guide *Western Whitewater* reports some outfitters have called it Green River Wilderness.

Now, in defense of the name *Desolation*, the first 40 miles—starting about 20 above Sand Wash and continuing for about 20 downstream—are very desolate. Wild mustangs wander around a barren desert with all the enthusiasm of teenagers on a family vacation. Other than the riparian rim of vegetation, the landscape is cast in pale brown, beige, and taupe. If you see some ocher, it's an absolute barn burner. Meanwhile, the final 20 miles through Gray Canyon are exactly as advertised—there's a quiet grace to the plainness, broken only by class II boulder garden rapids. But the lower 35 miles of Deso—from above Lighthouse Rock to below Three Fords Rapid, where the Tavaputs just falls away like the canyon exhausted itself from too much cool stuff—is one of the best stretches of river for exploration along the Powell route—maybe anywhere.

The reddish, interbedded sandstones and shales of the Wasatch formation give the canyon walls of lower Deso the look of crumbly brick pyramids with a green mortar of juniper and fir. Everywhere you turn, there's another panel of intricate Fremont-culture

Like most rapids along the Powell route, Joe Hutch Rapids formed when a side canyon flash flooded, pushing boulders into the river, which constricted the main channel.

" . . . Crags and tower-shaped peaks are seen everywhere, and away above them, long lines of broken cliffs; and above and below the cliffs are pine forests . . . a few dwarf bushes are seen here and there clinging to rocks, and cedars grow in the crevices . . ." —John Wesley Powell

rock art to visit. Short hikes lead to all types of historic sites—an iron-prowed skiff, a mushroom rock, a pair of preserved ranches, a Denis Julien inscription, plus old cabins, including a moonshiner's hideout. Most of the left shore, from 6 miles below Sand Wash to Coal Creek is tribal land belonging to the Uintah and Ouray Indian Reservation. Visitors must obtain a hiking and camping permit from the Ute Tribe, details below. I've heard occasional paddlers boast of ignoring this requirement. Not cool.

There are many class II rapids in this segment, with a few that are class III at certain levels. Thus, this is a perfect run for paddlers transitioning to intermediate challenges. With raft support, it's a great first-time long-distance whitewater kayaking trip. Or a good stretch to improve one's rowing skills. Or a perfect introduction to week-long expedition boating. Or a great self-support kayaker proving ground. Options!

Duration: 83 miles from Sand Wash to Swaseys is the standard run, typically done in 5–8 days.

A "best-kept" secret, which paddlers are always blabbing about, is that it's not about just the paddling but about the places the boats can take you.

NOLS participants hike from the landing strip toward Sand Wash to launch on a week-long paddling course in Deso. KIRK RASMUSSEN/NOLS

Access: Start at Sand Wash (W39 50.42' / N109 54.83') or upstream in the Uinta Basin. Stop at Swaseys Beach (N39 6.74' / W110 6.55') or continue to Green River State Park (N38 59.32' / W110 9.02') and beyond.

Logistics: Most river runners opt for shuttle service from River Runners Transport or Wilkins Bus Lines (see page 65). A self-shuttle from Sand Wash to Swaseys, using Sand Wash Rd., US 191, I-70, and Hastings/Beach Rd., is 184 miles and takes 4 hours one way.

Many groups motor down at first to spend as much time in inner Deso, roughly from Lighthouse Rock, at mile 24, to Three Fords Rapid, at mile 59. That said, there is plenty to explore in quieter upper Deso and Gray Canyon.

Season and weather: Early spring–late fall. Due to the potential for ice, Deso is not commonly run in winter. Typical canyon weather, including frequent thunderstorms, is possible year round. The canyon rim reaches to over 9,000 feet in the heart of Deso, where the river elevation at Rock Creek is 4,500 feet.

Water level and character: Class II+ to III; harder at high-water. Gradient is 6 fpm from Lighthouse Rock down. For levels, use gauge USGS Green River at Green River, UT.

Challenges and safety: When receding waters create stagnant pools in upper Deso, typically during early to midsummer depending on runoff, mosquitoes can be ferocious. Bring bug-netting hats, protective clothing, and repellent. At Sand Wash, three enclosed "bug" huts can be reserved on recreation.gov for camping the night before your launch. On the river, up-canyon winds can make flatwater traverses challenging. Some raft groups bring stowable motors, primarily for the first 20 miles.

Boats: Any boat capable of class II-III whitewater will do.

Camping: Primitive, and plenty of options, many of which have been etched in by river runners.

Regulations, agencies, fees: The Bureau of Land Management manages this segment. Required equipment includes an approved toilet system, fire pan, and more. Find info at www.recreation.gov/wildernessAreaDetails.do?contractCode=NRSO&parkId= 72440] The river-left shore, from about 7 miles below Sand Wash to Coal Creek is Ute tribal land. Hiking and camping is allowed only with a permit, which can be bought online. Print and carry the receipt on the river as proof of permit, obtained here: www .utetribe.com/desolation-permit.html.

Maps: The best river-running map is *Belknap's Waterproof Desolation River Guide*.

This Fremont culture petroglyph panel is found near Flat Canyon at mile 32.

Highlights: Four miles down from Sand Wash, the river enters the first of a series of amphitheaters, including Sumner's, but which is it exactly? (Please see Deso/Solo on the following page.) • The iron-prowed skiff is on river-left, at mile 14, just upstream from Gold Hole. • Rock House Canyon on river-right, at mile 15.5, offers a short hike to petroglyph panel. • About 302 miles down the Powell route is Lighthouse Rock, site of a famous 1871 photo. • About mile 26.5, a short hike from a campsite on river-right leads to Mushroom Rock, a unique formation with petroglyphs. • Firewater Canyon on river-left (Ute hiking permit required), at mile 29.5, has a hike to a moonshiner's cabin. • A petroglyph panel, just upstream of Flat Canyon, is on river-right at mile 32, while a side hike up the side canyon leads to a stone arch. • Rock Creek, on river-right at mile 41.5, has all types of stuff, including a pristine creek, a 1.5-mile hike to petroglyphs, and the ruins of Rock Creek Ranch. • Three Canyon is on river-right at mile 46, with a half-moon butte rising in circular valley. • In a boulder field on river-left near Chandler Creek, about mile 48.5, trapper Denis Julien carved his initials into a large rock in the 1830s. • At mile 56, the McPherson Ranch, with old

DESO/SOLO; OR SEARCHING FOR SUMNER'S AMPHITHEATER

Part I: Solo trip or death sentence? • an eclipse on the river • just some regular old symmetry-focused topographic detective work.

On the beach at Sand Wash, I'd been chatting with a dude, let's call him "Guy," about the first expeditions down the Green and Colorado Rivers. For over 2 hours.

"So you're a Powell fella," he'd observed. Our kindred spirits took it from there, as we chatted about books, theories, and favorite tales—all colored by Guy's tendency to swear like a sailor at a spelling bee.

Suddenly, we realized the time, having become so caught up in a shared passion. An eclipse was coming. At Guy's suggestion, my aim was to watch from a symmetrical amphitheater, 5 miles downstream. He'd spent a previous eclipse there, saying the shadow between dark and light swept across the canyon wall with a startling shimmer. But also, from his own research, he believed this might be the real Sumner's Amphitheater. A spot named in 1869 by John Wesley Powell's first expedition, but possibly placed incorrectly on maps by entirely different personnel during the second expedition in 1871. A looming eclipse, a cartographic controversy, a solo trip for 90 miles down Desolation and Gray Canyons of the Green River? Um, yes, please.

As I was preparing to push off from shore, Guy mentioned a few details about my upcoming run. In what felt like a minute-long sentence, without so much as a hard stop, Guy rattled off the basics about river toilet, firepan, and camping regs, before transitioning to a few warnings:

"There's big storms coming in, so watch out for lightning strikes in the river canyon, not much shelter but you'll probably be fine . . . be careful when hiking, even a sprained ankle can be a death sentence on a solo trip . . . hey, a lot of people say never go alone, but I think that's a crock of shit . . . look, we've had many black bear sightings lately, just don't surprise them and you should be okay . . . and some of the rapids rearranged during the spring high-water so just keep your eyes open for sneaker holes . . . oh and watch out for the wild mustangs, they might try to charge you onshore . . . it's more about you letting them show they've got the biggest balls . . . just don't show any fear, but don't be overconfident . . . don't move toward them, but don't move away either . . . and whatever you do, don't stand still—I can't really explain it."

I gulped. Luckily, I was rowing an insulated rubber raft with an SUP along for some side excursions from camps. Also, I'd sprained my ankles so many times, it's sort of a ligament-free-zone down there. I have a tendency to talk to myself out loud while walking, so that should scare off the bears like it normally does pedestrians. And the wild horses? Grazing on the ridges above, they seemed pretty peaceful. With a wave, I called out to Guy: "No zombies?"

Guy cupped his palm to his ear, then waved.

And I was off! This trip was the final major section in my multiyear project to explore the entire John Wesley Powell route. And to do it all as a fresh-eyes descent, meaning no one on the trip has seen that section of river before. This gives the trip a real exploratory feel, a bit like the Powell expeditions might have felt, granted much less so. Self-guided first times can also cause hilarious mistakes. Early the first morning of our fresh-eyes winter Grand Canyon trip, I mistook raven shit for toothpaste before ranger inspection at Lees Ferry. I spent a bewildered minute trying to bucket rinse it off the beach. Self-guided trips can also amplify the anxiety of the unknown. Usually I went with small groups of friends, but sometimes I went alone. This week-long class II+ trip, through one of the Powell route's most remote canyons, would be my longest solo yet.

An hour of rowing later, I tied up in the spot Guy had described, grabbed my eclipse "go-kit" (a brown bottled beer), and hiked up a crumbling ridgeline. In a meadow below, a small herd of grazing mustangs glanced up. I inhaled sharply as they began trotting up the hillside toward me. Thinking back on Guy's mentoring, I decided my best course of action was to walk a chaotic and zigzagging course—like I was lost in an airport or evading sniper fire. I dropped in and out of ravines, sometimes moving toward the horses, sometimes away. The mustangs stopped and looked around, puzzled. I think one lifted a hoof to scratch its temple.

Checking out the upstream view in Duches Hole at mile 4.5, which may be the real Sumner's Amphitheater.

The eclipse was soon, the orange-brown cliffs dimming to gray, but one complication. No eclipse glasses. I'd gone to dozens of stores on my drive to put-in, all sold out. The whole trip had been last minute. Only a few weeks before, after casually mentioning my passion project on the Powell route, I'd been hired by FalconGuides to turn it into an inspirational guidebook for the entire route, in full color with plenty of photos. Suddenly, the lone remaining section loomed as a major gap in my explorations. So, I'd grabbed a cancelation permit on a week's notice and driven to Utah. I'd invited plenty of friends as a longshot. As I drove toward put-in, I was still getting messages like "You're not going alone, are you?" No, I'd replied but didn't explain my only companions would be a huge pile of books about the expeditions.

Clouds wafted into the canyon just as the eclipse reached its peak. The beam of shadow and light Guy had described passed with an indefinite glimmer and was gone. As colors returned from a brightening sky, I considered Guy's claims. The naming of the amphitheater is not mentioned in any of the original journal entries of the expedition members. But in Powell's 1875 account, he describes sweeping "around curve after curve with almost continuous walls for several miles." In the previous sentence, he writes, "One of these we find very symmetrical and name it Sumner's Amphitheater." A few years later, the second expedition came down the river, using notes from the first expedition to help create a detailed map. In his 1925 book, *A Canyon Voyage*, crew member Frederick Dellenbaugh describes standing on a ridge where the river seemed just a stone's throw to either side.

The downstream portion of the amphitheater in Duches Hole looks pretty symmetrical. Read about the mystery in Deso/Solo, and check it out next time you're there!

Wild mustangs roam the banks of upper Desolation Canyon.

What he calls Sumner's Amphitheater "was perhaps one thousand feet high, beautifully carved by the rains and winds."

Standing on a cliff, 5 miles upstream of the one named for Sumner, this amphitheater looked damn symmetrical. The top was completely flat, the geologic strata parallel and mostly cohesive. In the downstream half of the curve, ridgelines began to emerge with pillars and hoodoos at regular intervals. The height was around 500 feet. The next test was to visit the other amphitheater for a little topographic detective work.

Downstream, I rowed for several miles through a second amphitheater and into the third, officially designated as Sumner's. On the map, this third meander had a more curved course in the river. But from water level, the rim appeared broken and uneven, the ridges crumbly and erratic. On the western side, a whole drainage ravine cut down from rim to river. There was little symmetry about it. Certainly, the inside bend matched Dellenbaugh's description of a narrow neck where one might toss rocks into the river on either side. And the cliffs were taller here, a few hundred feet short of a thousand. Perhaps Dellenbaugh and the second expedition had simply gone to the wrong spot for some reason or mixed the two up in both maps and memory? I continued downstream, finding myself in agreement with the observant Guy at Sand Wash.

Deso/Solo continues on candk.me/deso-solo2 or mikebezemek.com with Part II: A hidden inner canyon • intimate encounters with lightning • imagined conversations with historical figures • the myth of Old Brigham

COMMERCIAL OUTFITTERS FOR DESO/GRAY

All outfitters offer some variation of 4- to 6-day trips by raft and inflatable kayak.

Adventure Bound USA: 4–6 days; (800) 423-4668; adventureboundusa.com.

American River Touring Association: 6-day; (800) 323-2782; www.arta.org.

Colorado River & Trail Expeditions: 5-day; (801) 261-1789; www.crateinc.com.

Holiday Expeditions: 5–6 days; (800) 624-6323; www.bikeraft.com.

OARS: 5-day; (800) 346-6277; www.oars.com.

Sherri Griffith Expeditions: 5–6 days; (800) 332-2439; www.griffithexp.com.

Adrift Adventures of Canyonlands (formerly Tag-a-Long): 5-day; (435) 259-8594; www.adrift.net.

Western River Expeditions: 5-day; (866) 904-1160; www.westernriver.com.

National Outdoor Leadership School (NOLS) offers various paddling, rowing, and kayaking courses that include trips through Deso (www.nols.edu).

and new buildings, is on river-left. • Perhaps the hardest rapid on the run, Three Fords Rapids is a class III that marks the division between Deso and Gray Canyons. • At mile 69, Coal Creek enters on river-left, signally a long class II+ rapid and the ruins of an old homestead at the base of the cliffs. • Queen Nefertiti Rock at the start for the daily run cuts a striking image. • Swayseys Beach makes a great hangout spot before the trip ends. • Gunnison Butte is across the river about 361 miles down the modern Powell route.

Deso was designated a National Historic Landmark on the 100th anniversary of the 1869 expedition. Try to top that, 2019.

PADDLING: NEFERTITI TO SWASEYS (GREEN RIVER DAILY)

This section is also called Green River Daily, offering an 8-mile day trip with pool-drop class II–II+ rapids. Paddlers often come from nearby population centers for whitewater kayaking or day-trip rafting. The scenery in lower Gray Canyon is somewhat stark but has a rugged desert beauty before ending near the iconic Gunnison Butte at the Book Cliffs.

There are options for explorations and camping along the right shore, while river-left has a gravel road that parallels the road and allows for easy shuttles. While some

Looking downstream at Gray Canyon from near Coal Creek rapid. Note the homesteader's cabin. And that lone cottonwood, which I swear wasn't there a moment ago.

Late nineteenth century on Air Bed n' Bathless: "Rustic cabin-like experience in Gray Canyon. Excellent scenery! Amazing privacy. Abundant river water with great siltation possibilities. You provide own door, windows, and shade. We'll take any offer."

river trips may end Deso trips at Nefertiti, the access road and ramp are gravel, meaning most opt for the paved ramp and road access provided at Swaseys.

Duration: 8 miles; 3–5 hours.

Access: Start at the gravel boat ramp at Nefertiti access (N39 11.72' / W110 4.63'). End at Swaseys Beach boat ramp (N39 6.74' / W110 6.55'). Some paddlers choose to take out at the actual Swaseys Beach, which is on river-left, 0.25 mile upstream from the boat ramp.

Logistics: A self-shuttle using Hastings Rd./Beach Rd. is a straight shot on a riverside gravel road for 8 miles, which will take about 25 minutes.

Camping: Primitive camping is allowed at Nefertiti access, where there is a pit toilet. Primitive camping is allowed throughout the section, which is Bureau of Land Management land. Swaseys Beach Campground offers first-come sites and vault toilets for a fee.

PADDLING: SWASEYS TO GREEN RIVER STATE PARK

This section is a fine flatwater day trip with two complications that may have limited overall use by paddlers. First, there is a river-wide diversion dam at Tusher Wash, which at one time necessitated portaging. But today there is a boat chute that has been

A red-tailed hawk soars over Rock House Canyon, where there are also great rock formations and petroglyphs and polite signs of bears.

An invasive carp rises to the surface to feed in an eddy.

added to the center of the channel. Second, the banks are mostly private property, as the river winds through irrigated farm fields in a wide basin. While day trips do happen, the section is more commonly an add-on to extend a Deso trip by camping near Swaseys and continuing to Green River town the next day. Or it serves as a connector for through-paddlers continuing into Labyrinth Canyon.

Duration: 12.5 miles; 4–7 hours.

Access: Start at Swaseys Beach boat ramp (N39 6.74' / W110 6.55'). End at Green River State Park (N38 59.32' / W110 9.02').

Logistics: A self-shuttle between Swaseys and the state park, using Beach Rd./Hasting Rd., Business US 191/E. Main St., and Green River Blvd., takes 11 miles and 20 minutes one way.

Camping: There is a primitive campground at Swaseys Beach and a landscaped campground at Green River State Park, with showers and a small store.

6

LABYRINTH AND
STILLWATER CANYONS

IF YOU EVER HAVE THE FORTUNE OF FLYING ACROSS THE UNITED STATES along roughly the 38th parallel, make sure you have a window seat. Below you spreads one of the most unique regions on our planet. An area of sunken canyons, sharp cliffs, deep slots, and hidden alcoves carved into rock like a baker cutting up a sandstone sheet cake. There are intriguing names like Bowknot Bend, Tower Park, White Rim, Hardscrabble Bottom, and Island in the Sky. Sounds more like the stuff of fantasy literature than paddling adventure.

In fact, during 2017, NASA posted a photo taken from space to their Instagram feed—which typically includes images of icy moons or black holes—with the comment "Is this reddish landscape on another world or right here on Earth?" The image, with southeast at the top, didn't show Mars but the sinuous curves of the Green River winding past the meteorite-impact remnants of Upheaval Dome toward its confluence with the similarly shaped Colorado River. Yeah, you should probably paddle through all this.

The section called Labyrinth (the actual canyon continues below Mineral Bottom) is 45 miles, managed by the Bureau of Land Management, and has a self-issue permit. With road access to a pair of put-ins and a single take-out, it's the more commonly paddled section. The section called Stillwater (which begins in lower Labyrinth Canyon) flows mostly through Canyonlands National Park, has no lottery but requires a call-in or online permit in advance, and necessitates either arranging a jet boat pickup from the confluence or continuing through the next segment, class III–IV Cataract Canyon. As a result, Stillwater sees less overall river traffic, though neither section, being so remote, is particularly crowded.

Calling these canyons flatwater does a disservice in two ways. First, with side hikes, ruins, rock art, and some of the best geologic scenery along the entire Powell route, this segment is anything but boring. And second, it's a little rude to other flatwater

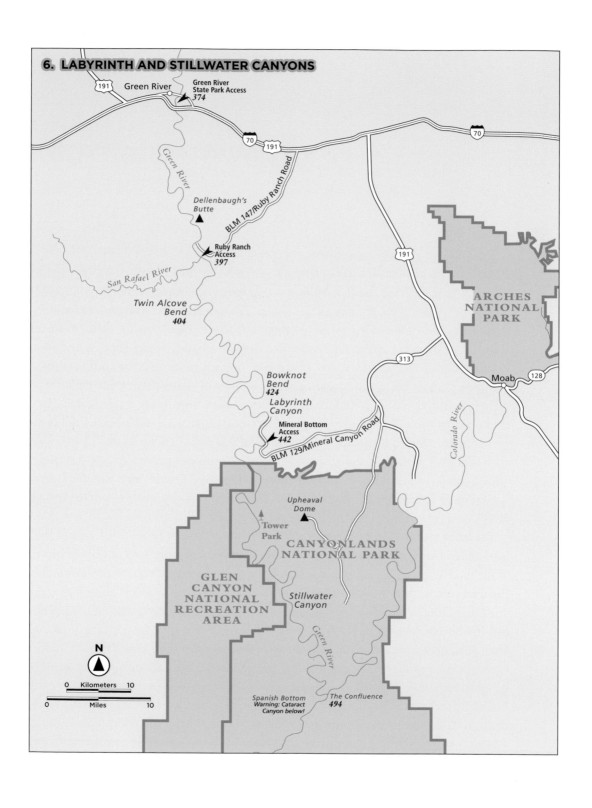

6. LABYRINTH AND STILLWATER CANYONS

191

Green River

Green River
State Park Access
374

70 191

Green River

BLM 147/Ruby Ranch Road

Dellenbaugh's
Butte
▲

191

70

ARCHES
NATIONAL
PARK

Ruby Ranch
Access
397

San Rafael River

Twin Alcove
Bend
404

313

Moab

128

Bowknot
Bend
424

Labyrinth
Canyon

Colorado River

Mineral Bottom
Access
442

BLM 129/Mineral Canyon Road

Upheaval
Dome
▲

Tower
Park

CANYONLANDS
NATIONAL PARK

GLEN
CANYON
NATIONAL
RECREATION
AREA

Stillwater
Canyon

Green River

N

0   Kilometers   10

0   Miles   10

Spanish Bottom
Warning: Cataract
Canyon below!

The Confluence
494

Turks Head is one of the most recognizable rock formations along the entire Powell route, found roughly 452 paddling miles from Green River, WY.

rivers because most flatwater rivers have *some* current. This water seems to almost move upstream at times. But what you give out in effort, you more than make up for with experience. While Dino offers mind-bending folds, and Deso offers surprising complexity, and the Grand offers endless depths and variety, Lab and Stillwater offer a casual intimacy. The rim always seems within reach and is always changing, including the varnished Navajo sandstone, the startling White Rim sandstone, or spires capped by Wingate sandstone in Tower Park, which resembles a riverside Monument Valley. So, yeah, you should probably paddle through all this.

Duration: The entire segment, from Green River State Park to the confluence with the Colorado River, is 120 miles and would take 6–10 days. Ruby Ranch to confluence is 97 miles, 5–9 days. The short estimates are more realistic at higher water levels, which accelerate the current. See sections below for further discussion and specific access information.

Much of Labyrinth Canyon feels like the Green River passes through a mini Monument Valley.

Logistics: Because of the slow dirt roads leading to Ruby Ranch and Mineral Bottom, most groups hire a shuttle service (see list below). If you are unable or unwilling to continue through the whitewater of Cataract, you'll need to arrange for extraction by jet boat outfitter, for people and equipment, up the Colorado River to Moab, UT. To connect with vehicles, further shuttles are typically available. ***Note:*** Combining segments 6 and 7 creates a great 10- to 14-day trip of 168 miles with a self-shuttle, between Green River State Park and Dirty Devil access on Lake Powell, of only 1.5 hours each way.

Season and weather: Early spring–late fall. Most don't say year round because the river can have ice during winter, but people do go, depending on their comfort with the conditions. Average annual precipitation is around 7 inches, so you can leave your portable cisterns at home. Spring daytime temps are fairly warm (60°F–80°F) with cold nights (30°F–45°F), while summer daytime temps approach 100°F, with nights in the 60s.

Water level and character: Bring your bubble levels because the water is flat flat flat. Class I, with a bit of I+ if you're lucky. The gradient is roughly 2 fpm. If ever there were a river to use the designation I-, this may be it. Use gauge USGS Green River at Green River, UT.

This spot goes by several names—5 Window Arch, 5 Hole Arch, and Colonnade Arch. Whatever it's called, it's definitely a favorite side hike up a steep trail at Two Mile Canyon, below Bowknot Bend in Labyrinth Canyon.

RIVER MAPS AND GUIDES FOR CANYONLANDS AREA

There are three popular options that cover Segment 6: Labyrinth and Stillwater Canyons and Segment 7: Cataract Canyon. The first two are more focused on topographic maps for navigation while supplementing with facts and information. The latter option is more focused on facts and information and, as of the 2012 edition, includes nontopographic reference maps.

Belknap's Waterproof Canyonlands River Guide

RiverMaps' *Guide to the Colorado & Green Rivers in the Canyonlands of Utah & Colorado*

River Guide to Canyonlands National Park and Vicinity by Michael Kelsey

OUTFITTERS, SERVICES, AND GUIDES FOR LAB AND STILLWATER

Canyon Voyages Adventure Co. offers guided kayak trips down Labyrinth Canyon, plus a wide variety of boat and equipment sales and rentals; (866) 390-3994; www.canyonvoyages.com.

Coyote Shuttle offers vehicle transfers and full service shuttles for runs on Labyrinth and Stillwater; (435) 260-2097; www.coyoteshuttle.com.

Moab Rafting & Canoe Company offers guided canoe trips and self-guided canoe rentals through Labyrinth and Stillwater Canyons. They will also transport people and boats to and from various access points; (435) 259-7722; moab-rafting.com.

NAVTEC Expeditions offers guided 4-day raft-supported kayak trips through Labyrinth, 4-day trips through Stillwater & Cataract, plus raft, motor rig, ducky, and other equipment rentals; (800) 833-1278; navtec .com.

Sherri Griffith Expeditions offers 5-day guided kayaking trips, plus their 12-day John Wesley Powell theme trip also goes through; (800) 332-2439; www.griffithexp.com.

Tex's Riverways rents canoes and kayaks for self-guided trips through Labyrinth and Stillwater Canyons. They offer vehicle shuttles for both runs, and a jet boat shuttle is available for taking out at the confluence; (877) 662-2839; texsriverways.com.

Challenges and safety: The main challenge here is carrying enough drinking water. The river is very silty and stagnant through here, meaning most river groups prefer to bring their own water rather than filtering or treating.

Boats: You can get anything down this stretch if you have the time and patience. Long kayaks, SUPs, rafts, canoes, inflatable lounge chairs. If it floats on water, yes, this is water.

Camping. There are no official sites, but many have been established by boaters. At low water, you can camp on plenty of sandbars and beaches. At higher water, it gets trickier. High-ground spots can be few and far between, so start looking early in the afternoon. I strongly suggest you offer to share with other boaters coming down-stream, because this might very well be you the next day.

Supplies. Green River, UT, or Moab.

Highlights: How much time do you have? Crystal Geyser on river-left, about 5 miles below state park. • About 392 miles down the route, Dellenbaugh Butte is on river-left, a favorite site of the 1871 expedition member. • Trin Alcove Bend is 7 miles downstream from Ruby Ranch. • Hey Joe Canyon, on river-left about 21 miles below Ruby Ranch, has a short hike to an abandoned uranium mine. • About 425 miles below Green River, WY, begins Bowknot Bend, which takes 8 miles to return to a spot 1,000' to the south. • A series of landings on river-right allow access to a trail leading up the north side of the "neck" to the saddle above. • About 53 miles from Ruby, Upheaval Bottom can be reached by a river-left trail after 4 miles one way. • Three miles downstream, at Fort Bottom, the inner bend has an old log cabin on a low bluff and an ancestral Puebloan ruin on a tall bluff. • The startling White Rim sandstone and Tower Park begin soon after. • Turks Head is one of the quirkier and more recognizable rock formations along the Powell route, about 470 miles down. • The river enters Stillwater Canyon about 33 miles below Mineral Bottom. • At Jasper Canyon, on river-right about 10 miles into Stillwater, a short hike leads to a small ruins. • Finally, 120 miles from Green River, UT, and 494 miles from Expedition Island, the confluence with the Colorado River.

PADDLING: GREEN RIVER, UT, TO RUBY RANCH

The highlights of this section are floating past the manmade Crystal Geyser, the remarkably symmetrical Dellenbaugh's Butte, and entering Labyrinth Canyon from its very scenic beginnings. Though it could be done alone, this section is probably best added on to the following section and maybe during higher-water trips.

Duration: 23 miles, 1–2 days. Moves fairly well at high-water.

"Many of these buttes were beautiful in their castellated form as well as because of a picturesque banded character, and opposite our dinner camp, which was on a ledge of rock, was one surprisingly symmetrical, resembling an artificial structure. I thought it looked like an art gallery, and the Major said it ought to be named after the artist, so he called it 'Dellenbaugh's Butte.'" —Frederick Dellenbaugh (located about 393 paddling miles down the route)

Access: Start at Green River State Park (N38 59.32' / W110 9.02'). Stop at Ruby Ranch (N38 46.64' / W110 6.31') or continue downriver through Lab.

Logistics: A self-shuttle from Green River State Park to Ruby Ranch, using I-70 and gravel Ruby Ranch Rd., is 1 hour each way.

Regulations, agencies, fees: There are small access fees at both the state park and Ruby Ranch. There is no permit needed for these 23 miles, but trips continuing through Lab will need one (info below).

PROFESSOR LEADS EXPEDITION DOWN THE POWELL ROUTE FOR SESQUICENTENNIAL REDISCOVERY

Tom Minckley is an associate professor, studying environmental change and biogeography, in the Geography Department at the University of Wyoming. On May 24, 2019, his project, the Sesquicentennial Colorado River Exploring Expedition (SCREE) will launch from Green River, WY. His motley crew of scientists, artists, and policy makers will descend the entire route of John Wesley Powell's 1869 expedition, asking about how Powell's land settlement theories relate to the modern state of western resources. For more info, visit www.powell150.org.

Mike: So, what are the goals of your project?

Tom: Well, our trip is not a reenactment, where we use poorly equipped boats and eat rotten flour and sour coffee. Our project is largely defined by the impact of John Wesley Powell on the West. We're going to boat the whole thousand miles in one shot to engage in a dialogue about the future of the arid West in light of decreasing water supplies, degrading landscapes, and increasing populations, and a host of related cultural, economic, political, and social issues. We are interested in what people envision for the next 150 years in the American West. What do people want the future of the region to be for their children?

We want to get people on the river because it's a great place to talk. Nature and rivers tend to relax people and let them think philosophically. There are fewer distractions. I notice at resource meetings, we basically say the same things. In my classes, the students are afraid to be wrong. We're losing our ability to talk to each other. Yes, everyone is committed to the region, but the environment is changing faster than policy. The dialogue about the West and its resources needs an infusion of new ideas. We're stuck in the ways of the past, entrenched in our thinking about what is best, and not managing resources for the future. We are blinded to what could be and needs to be more creative.

Mike: How does John Wesley Powell come into the project?

Tom: It started from a group of us pondering to what extent the American West followed the agrarian settlement model proposed by John Wesley Powell. Powell is an adventurer in American lore, but he was really a bureaucrat and public servant after the expeditions. His agrarian settlement plan is detailed in *Across the Hundredth Meridian* by Wallace Stegner and *A River Running West* by Donald Worster. Powell believed the government would have to be involved with irrigating the land, and his plan was to map the region and determine the existing resources and proper governance of those resources for the people. But Powell's ideas were largely rejected and bypassed as the railroads sold off their lands and boosters promoted uncontrolled settlement within the arid region, possibly represented by the abandoned towns and cabins seen along the route today.

Powell believed that water reaching the ocean was wasted. His nephew, Arthur Davis Powell, became the first director of the US Reclamation Service. I can't believe that "Uncle Wes" didn't impart his ideas about damming and irrigation on his nephew. And what eventually happened in the West with water development partly resembles Powell's plan. Our hypothesis is that we ultimately live the legacy of JWP, through trial and error, but it took many decades to implement. On our trip, we want to gain clarity about that legacy and to consider whether it represents where we would like to see things go in the future. These days, we must also consider endangered species, recreation, and the aesthetic value of the land. Modern society is more complicated than in his time.

Mike: What do you hope comes out of your expedition?

Tom: Our crew will be a diverse group of scholars, artists, policy makers, and stakeholders, who are coming together to think widely about the Colorado River basin as a resource for all. We have a landscape painter, tintype photographer, and writers who will meet the region's residents and create works on the banks of the river. During our expedition, we will have a distributed art show along the Powell route, in Green River, WY; Green River, UT; Page, AZ; and Flagstaff, AZ. Afterward, the writing will be collected in a book, and the artwork will travel to other venues to reach the greater public and hopefully move the dialogue forward. The resources we depend on are diminishing, and we need to think proactively so we don't spend decades fighting over water, which Powell did warn us of. The Powell expedition was the last great adventure of American discovery. Now we need some rediscovery. We only get one sesquicentennial, so let's make it count.

This old log structure at Fort Bottom is described by some as an outlaw cabin.

PADDLING: LABYRINTH CANYON

Any random dictionary defines a labyrinth as "an intricate passageway or tortuous maze—" Oh, just go and see it for yourself already!

Duration: 45 miles; 3–5 days.

Access: Start at Ruby Ranch (N38 46.64' / W110 6.31') or upstream. End at Mineral Bottom (N38 31.49' / W109 59.60') or continue downstream (requires jet boat pickup or continuing into Cataract).

Logistics: Most trips opt for a shuttle service. A self-shuttle from Ruby Ranch to Mineral Bottom using Ruby Ranch Rd., I-70, US 191, UT 313, and BLM 129, takes

This Ancestral Puebloan watchtower sits on a bluff at Fort Bottom.

70 miles and 2 hours each way. The self-shuttle from Green River State Park is 1.5 hours each way.

Regulations, agencies, fees: A Lab trip passes through Bureau of Land Management lands. A self-issue permit must be completed and one copy e-mailed to BLM (blm_ut_labyrinth@blm.gov) and one copy carried on the trip. The free permit is hopefully still here: www.blm.gov/download/file/fid/14487 or here: www.blm.gov/tag/labyrinth-canyon, otherwise google it. BLM has regulations for river runners, including required use of portable toilet system, maximum group size of 25, and approved firepan at least 12" wide be carried on all overnight trips.

PADDLING: STILLWATER CANYON

One thing alone makes this trip worth it —the White Rim. All the other great things are just a bonus.

Duration: 52 miles; 3-5 days.

Access: Start at Mineral Bottom (N38 31.49' / W109 59.60') or upstream; take out at confluence with Colorado River by scheduled jet boat (see logistics) or continue into Cataract Canyon (class III–IV).

The White Rim sandstone steals the show in lower Labyrinth Canyon, but oddly Powell barely even mentions it in his 1875 account. Just too much to pick from, I guess.

A side hike up Stove Canyon in Stillwater, after a rain, reveals hundreds of water pockets, which the Powell expeditions used for drinking water during their side explorations. MAX GANS

Logistics: Most flatwater paddlers who run Stillwater work with a shuttle service or outfitter, given the need for a jet boat ride out from the confluence. If you continue through Cataract, you'll need to self-shuttle from Mineral Bottom to Dirty Devil, using BLM 129, UT 313, US 191, I-70, UT 24, and UT 95, which takes 3 hours and 170 miles one way.

Regulations, agencies, fees: A Stillwater trip passes through Canyonlands National Park, which requires a flatwater permit, fees, and following of regulations similar to those listed for Lab, above. All can be obtained here: www.nps.gov/cany/planyour visit/riverpermits.htm.

1869, PART IV: LET'S GO NAME COOL STUFF IN CANYONLANDS!

I like my geology how I like my jaybirds • 10,000 strangely carved forms • the confluence at last! • a mystery of the rocks • will we do any boating on this lovely portaging trip?

Below Gunnison Butte, the expedition entered a wide basin of hot winds and blowing sand. To the south, Sumner saw snowcapped peaks, which he called the Uncompahgre Mountains, but they were probably the La Sal Mountains, which rise near present-day Moab. They passed some mineral spring deposits, today called Crystal Geyser. Next came symmetrical buttes of gypsum that, in a few years, would be named for the artist on the second expedition, Frederick Dellenbaugh.

Gradually, a new canyon appeared, with bluffs and low walls of orange sandstone. The river was calm as a lake, and the hot sun baked the men inside a bedrock oven. On July 15, they camped at a bend in the river, where three side canyons cut down into the canyon walls to create an alcove—so they named this Trin Alcove Bend. Where the river made a sweeping bend for 8 miles before returning to within 1,000 feet of the upstream channel became Bowknot Bend. Towers of rock were passed in a section that became Tower Park. A butte like a fallen cross was named as such, even after discovering it was two buttes they'd visually merged from upstream perspective. The deepening canyon was so tortuous, it was named Labyrinth.

Powell was swept up in this landscape of naked rock. His endless desire for cataloging showed in his descriptions of cones, buttresses, columns, alcoves, cliffs, tables, plateaus, terraces, crags, and "ten thousand strangely carved forms." These bare and polished rocks were white, gray, red, brown, and chocolate. Though the men wrote little of this region, Powell believed they were similarly enthralled, and they occasionally discharged a pistol to hear the echoing reports. Sumner's few notes were particularly focused on food, including catching a single beaver and one goose from a flock they'd prompted down the river for 3 days.

An 1871 view of Trin Alcove Bend from across the river; J. K. Hillers. US GEOLOGICAL SURVEY

As the river entered a more coherent walled-in landscape and the current continued to languish, a new name was declared, Stillwater Canyon. After 20 miles, they reached the long anticipated confluence with the Grand River. Here, the two rivers combined in what Powell called "solemn depths, more than 1,200 feet below the general surface of the country." They'd come over 500 miles in 53 days, about halfway down their route. Below flowed the Colorado River, their conveyance to the Grand Canyon.

The men were excited to reach this milestone, especially given the river flowed calm and stately despite doubling in volume. It wasn't the "rushing, roaring mountain torrent" of waterfalls and cataracts that Bradley had been told to expect, though he did ponder if the placid waters might lead to a disastrous canyon of death. The men camped on the point of land between the Green and Grand Rivers and focused on completing chores and washing clothes. While inspecting the rations, they found the flour lumpy and water-damaged. After sifting it through mosquito netting, they were compelled to throw away a quarter, leaving only about 600 pounds. To supplement their similarly dwindling bacon, they caught two beavers, which made excellent but heavy soup.

That's right—E. O. Beaman hauled his camera up to the saddle of Bowknot Bend in 1871.
US GEOLOGICAL SURVEY

The original plan was to layover at the confluence for nearly 3 weeks to observe an eclipse, but given the diminished rations, they stayed about 5 days. This was long enough to climb the cliffs in 100-degree heat and record lat/long for the confluence, which had never been certain to within 100 miles on American maps. On July 21, they started downriver, encountering rapids within 2 miles. To protect the rations, they ran very few, even some they felt comfortable with. This latest canyon was a new type of rugged, stripped of vegetation at river level and crumbly. A confusion of rocks, as Powell called it. For a camp, they found no flat ground, so they made beds by piling rocks along the edge of the water and collected what sand they could to fill the cracks.

After a second day of mostly portaging in what became Cataract Canyon, the men made oars while the hungry cook, Hawkins, used the instruments to determine coordinates for the nearest pie. Powell and his brother, Walter, climbed a mountain above camp to unravel the mystery of the rocks. Powell correctly observed the river cut across an anticlinal axis, essentially where bedrock below had domed upward, causing the surrounding canyon walls to fault into blocks, which slid bottoms-out into the river. This collapsing of the cliffs was what created the many dangerous rapids. Another

The water in Cataract Canyon rapid moved too swiftly for J. K. Hillers's camera in 1871.
US Geological Survey

mystery, Sumner found fresh moccasin prints on a sandy beach but never saw an owner.

Over the next few days, they encountered dozens of rapids in quick succession. Hours were spent carrying the freight boats over huge boulders onshore. Few rapids were run, and most portages required challenging ferries from one side of the river to the other. When Oramel broke an oar in one such crossing, he was nearly pulled into the rapid below. Sumner believed it would smash any boat to pieces, writing, "God help the poor wretch that is caught in the cañon during highwater." For an hour one night, Powell sat watching the massive waves build into ridges and collapse into foam. The whitewater-enthused Bradley had his own view. Noting the high-water mark often stood 15–20 feet above the current level, he believed "there must be fun here when it is at that [height]."

Eventually they portaged around what today are called the Big Drop rapids. Bradley wrote, "We have met nothing to compare with it before." Below, the rapids eased, but before they could resume river running, the boats were beaten and leaking. They'd lost many oars along the way. From camp on river-left, Powell and four men climbed a side canyon—possibly called Gypsum today—in search of pitch, or tree sap, to patch the boats. Only Powell returned with any, about 2 pounds, collected in the unused sleeve for his missing right arm.

Periodic rapids resumed downstream, including occasional bad ones that required portaging, but their progress increased. The canyon walls lowered and narrowed, so this became Narrow Canyon. And on July 28, they entered a wide valley near a previously unknown stream. According to Sumner, the water was "as filthy as the washing from the sewers of some large, dirty city, but stinks more than cologne ever did." Powell named it the Dirty Devil River, a somewhat controversial name because it may have been meant as an insult for at least one of the mountain men and perhaps drew ire from some of the others.

The 1869 adventure continues on page 171 . . .

CATARACT CANYON

BIG DESERT RIVERS IN THE SOUTHWEST HAVE A WAY ABOUT THEM. Despite countless efforts to "tame" them like beasts of burden—through dams, diversions, species swaps, and flow alterations—the rivers still manage to do roughly what they want. It might take some distance, from a few dozen to a few hundred miles, for the river to regain a sediment load or some semblance of a natural hydrograph, but eventually it goes back to being itself—granted, in a diminished state. Nowhere along the Powell route can this be more readily observed by paddlers than in 15 upper miles of Cataract Canyon.

The famous danger sign, 3 miles below the confluence, is also an important campsite sign-up location.

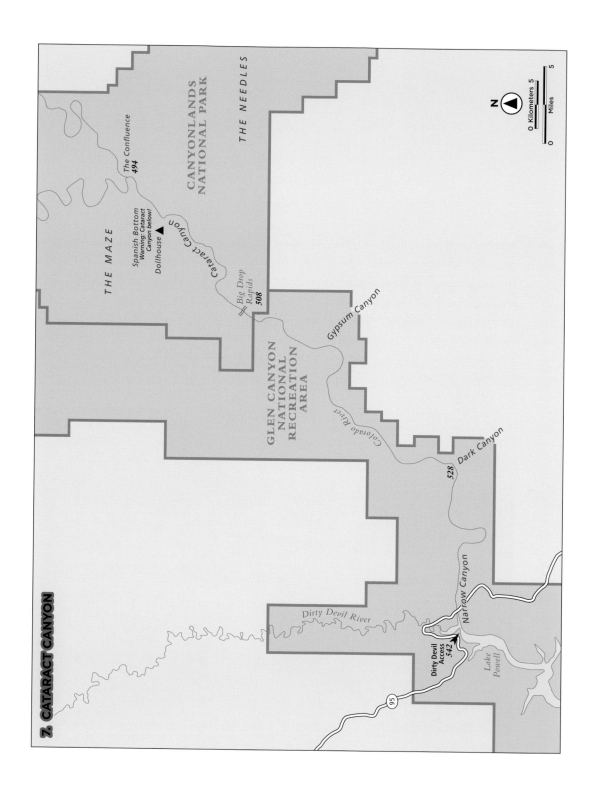

7. CATARACT CANYON

THE MAZE

CANYONLANDS NATIONAL PARK

THE NEEDLES

The Confluence
494

Spanish Bottom
*Warning: Cataract
Canyon below!*
Dollhouse

Cataract Canyon

Big Drop
Rapids
508

Gypsum Canyon

GLEN CANYON
NATIONAL
RECREATION
AREA

Colorado River

Dark Canyon

528

Narrow Canyon

Dirty Devil River

Dirty Devil
Access
542

Lake
Powell

95

N

0 Kilometers 5
0 Miles 5

Take the Big Drops, for example. At high water, these are the biggest rapids on the Powell route and some argue the biggest whitewater (more in terms of volume and power, not gradient and danger) that is regularly and commercially run in the United States. Those features, with names like Little Niagara, Purgatory, and Satan's Gut, occur just over 400 miles downstream from Flaming Gorge Dam, the nearest major upstream impoundment on the Green River, while the closest on the Colorado River is the Price-Stubb Diversion Dam about 180 miles upstream near Grand Junction, CO.

OARS guide Lars Haarr drops a dory through explosive waves at Big Drop I (about 507 paddling miles down the route) in Cataract Canyon. Check out more great adventure photography at www.justinbailie.com. JUSTIN BAILE

A wave crashes over a dory during an OARS trip through Cataract Canyon at high water. To get this amazing shot, adventure photographer and guidebook author James Kaiser rigged a GoPro to take automatic exposures. See more at www.jameskaiser.com. JAMES KAISER

In late spring every year, the flows in Cat often exceed 20,000–30,000 cfs. In wet years, high flows might peak at over 50,000 cfs. Online, you can find stories and videos of descents at even higher flows of 60,000, 80,000, and even 100,000 cfs during the high-water years in the early 1980s. Today, 15 miles of rapids remain in what was the most chaotic canyon not called Grand on the Powell route. Today, the lower miles of Cat and all of Narrow Canyon are flooded by Lake Powell. In recent decades, the reservoir has receded substantially. The result is the curious site of loose lake sediments that line the shore. These cliffs of mud and silt occasionally crumble from the wakes of passing motorboats and tumble into the waters below, reminding paddlers of the tremendous changes to the Powell route since the introduction of large dams.

In addition to whitewater, there are several great highlights to a Cataract trip: first, access to the Maze or Needles In Canyonlands, including the remarkable Dollhouse from Spanish Bottom. In Narrow Canyon, depending on water level, paddlers can divert up Dark Canyon in boats and possibly on foot, depending on the presence of mud where water ends. While Cataract is a great trip that sees a steady stream of visitors, the remote and challenging character, combined with lengthy entries down the Green or Colorado Rivers, means the river is rarely overcrowded.

Duration: 47.5 miles and 3–6 days, depending if you tow or row the final 27 miles on upper Lake Powell, for Cat and

Narrow only. And remember, you must enter from upstream sections, meaning a minimum 100-mile trip.

Access: Start upstream on the Green River (see Segment 6) or Colorado River (see other paddling, below). End at Dirty Devil access (N37 53.29' / W110 24.04') on Lake Powell.

Logistics: Most private groups running Cat come down the Colorado River side because of easier access from Moab. Powell pilgrims committed to the route can start from Mineral Bottom, Ruby Ranch, Green River State Park, or upstream. During high water, some groups will hire a motor support boat from companies out of Moab, which can run safety through the whitewater and motor out across the reservoir.

Season and weather: Early spring–late fall; winter trips do happen, but beware of ice on the flatwater entry sections. Weather is comparable to Segment 6. River-level elevation at the confluence is about 3,900'.

Water level and character: Most rapids are class III–III+/IV-, with the Big Drops and a few others ranking class IV–IV+ and perhaps V, with the upper classifications occurring at increasing water levels. Gradient in the whitewater section is 16 fpm. Water level is determined by adding two upstream gauges: USGS Green River at Green River, UT, and USGS Colorado River at Cisco, UT. American Whitewater provides a helpful graph in their online river-running database that automatically adds the two gauges.

Challenges and safety: There are many challenges on this segment, first of which is just getting down the flatwater. Once arrived, the rapids are big with powerful hydraulics that will toss around small craft and can flip even the biggest rafts in the right circumstances. High water just increases the power and chaos, but every year plenty of high-water junkies and commercial trips make the descent. Consider hiring a support boat to run safety for you through the rapids and provide a tow across upper Lake Powell. Regarding the reservoir, as of 2017, the final 27 miles are reservoir known for consistent up-canyon winds that funnel into paddlers' faces in Narrow Canyon.

Boats: The issue with this segment is that the boats ideal for the entry to flatwater tend to not be ideal for the rapids. For this reason, many raft trips are equipped with motors for the flats and oars for the rapids. High-volume whitewater kayaks are ideal, but some skilled through-paddlers take sea or touring kayaks through the rapids. Experienced packrafters go through mostly at lower flows. Paddle rafts also make the descent but should be prepared for possible flips and swims. Given the nature of the run and the variability of flows, this is very much a personal decision. In general, smaller means more maneuverable but less stable.

Why wouldn't you park your boat at a scenic spot like Spanish Bottom? Just a 500-mile paddle from Green River, WY.

Camping: There are designated campsites, which are first-come, first-served under a self-sign-up system. Stop at the courtesy camp sign-up box 2 miles below the confluence on river-left, near the infamous Danger sign. Camping is marginal for the last 27 miles, due to crumbly and high silt banks and fluctuating reservoir levels.

Supplies: Stores? This is about as far from supplies as you can get. Try Moab or Green River, UT.

Regulations, agencies, fees: Cataract Canyon is managed by Canyonlands National Park. A permit must be obtained in advance by phone or online. There is currently no daily launch limit; (435) 259-4351; www.nps.gov/cany.

Maps: *Belknap's Waterproof Canyonlands River Guide*; *RiverMaps Guide to the Colorado & Green Rivers in Canyonlands of Utah & Colorado*; *National Geographic* Trails Illustrated.

OUTFITTERS AND SERVICES FOR CATARACT CANYON

Companies offering equipment rental and shuttles at the top, followed by guided trips by oar and motor raft.

Coyote Shuttle offers vehicle transfers and full-service shuttles for Cataract trips originating on either the Green or Colorado Rivers; (435) 260-2097; www.coyoteshuttle.com.

NAVTEC Expeditions offers guided 4-day raft trips, plus raft, motor rig, ducky, and other equipment rentals; (800) 833-1278; navtec.com.

Redtail Air Adventures offers airplane shuttles for Cataract between Hite airstrip and Moab, plus van connections to other access points: (435) 259-7421; flyredtail.com.

Tex's Riverways offers a jet boat shuttle into CAT, which can take people and personal gear to meet private or commercial raft trips. Kayak transport also possible. (877) 662-2839; texsriverways.com.

Adrift Adventures of Canyonlands: 1–6 days by motor/oar raft; (435) 259-8594; www.adrift.net.

Adventure Bound USA: 2–7 days by motor/oar raft; (970) 245-5428; adventureboundusa.com.

Colorado River & Trail Expeditions: 3–10 days by motor/oar raft; (801) 261-1789; www.crateinc.com.

Holiday River Expeditions: 3–6 days by oar raft; (801) 266-2087; www.bikeraft.com.

OARS; 6 days by oar raft: (800) 346-6277; www.oars.com.

Sherri Griffith Adventures: 2–6 days by motor/oar raft, plus a 12-day JWP theme trip; (800) 332-2439; www.griffithexp.com.

Tour West: 3–4 days by motor/oar raft; (801) 225-0755; www.twriver.com/colorado-river-rafting.

Western River Expeditions: 2–4 days by motor/oar raft; (866) 904-1160; www.westernriver.com.

Wilderness River Adventure: 2–5 days by motor/oar raft; (800) 992-8022; www.riveradventures.com.

World Wide River Expeditions: 3–5 days by motor/oar raft; (435) 259-7515; www.worldwideriver.com.

A raft flotilla from Sherri Griffith Expeditions shows a popular method for motoring out from a Cat trip through the Narrow Canyon section of Lake Powell.

Highlights: Stop at the campsite sign-up board on river left, 2 miles below the confluence, plus get the obligatory photo. • Another mile and Spanish Bottom begins on right, with three campsites and access to day hikes up to the Doll's House. • Around mile 11.5, Range Canyon enters on river-right, creating a mile-long series of rapids, #13–19. • After a short break, rapid 20/Ben Hurt signals the need to eddy quickly on river-left to scout the Big Drops. • Big Drop Beach is at mile 13.5 and a 0.5-mile trail leads to Poop Rock, which is a random name and in no way suggestive of what may happen to your pants after getting a look at Big Drop 2. • Gypsum Canyon enters river-left about 20 miles down, and here is where the reservoir typically starts. • Mile 33.5 offers Dark Canyon on river-left, worth a visit. • Of course there's much more than rapids to discover.

Rock spires near the Dollhouse as seen from the river below.

OTHER PADDLING: MEANDER CANYON OF COLORADO RIVER THROUGH CANYONLANDS

Coming down Meander Canyon of the Colorado River through Canyonlands is the preferred entry side for most Cat trips, given it has easy river access in Moab, UT, where the commercial raft companies are based, or downstream at Potash Access. These starting points require boating down 64 or 47 river miles of flatwater, respectively, with similar cultural and historic sites, side hikes, and comparable scenery but different geology—mostly crimson sandstones, which give the river its name. All die-hard canyon country paddlers will want to visit this section.

LAKE POWELL AND GLEN CANYON

SPEND ENOUGH TIME IN THE SOUTHWEST, especially on the Colorado Plateau, and you'll learn that Lake Powell is a flash point for political, environmental, and recreational debate. Even just calling the reservoir a lake is too much for some critics, who emphatically refer to it as Reservoir Powell. Most river runners only see the remote, uppermost section of the reservoir in flooded Narrow Canyon while motoring out from a Cataract trip. Meanwhile, other paddlers explore side canyons, take overnight trips, or even through-paddle the entire lake—typically outside the main tourist season. Plus, there remain 15 miles of amazing paddling on the Colorado River through Glen Canyon. Starting a mile below the dam, this section provides a lofty reminder of the type of beauty that once extended for 150 miles upstream. With all this backstory, what's a paddler to do?

To start, don't just skip over Lake Powell without a second thought. Yes, like its name suggests, Lake Powell is a massive contradiction. It's a man-made freshwater sea that sits in a landscape of barren rock. The water is crystal clear, except for occasional oil films during high season from motorboat use. It's one of the two largest storage reservoirs in the United States, but it's usually only half full because it's located in an EFFing desert, guys, and one of the most sparsely populated regions in the country. Depending on time of year, you may see more flashing coeds than pictographs or ruins. It's clearly on the tourist trail, with a reported 3 million annual visitors coming from all over the world. Yet, even during high season, paddlers can usually find a quiet cove or inlet if they look hard enough. Nearby, the city of Page is a complex character, like a mini Los Angeles next to the big desert reservoir. All told, this area would make a great setting for a David Lynch–style miniseries—is the title *Twin Buttes* too on the nose?

If you do only one section from this segment, then make sure it's the 15 miles of river called the "backhaul." Since no road access is allowed near the dam, paddlers and their gear must be hauled on motorboats upstream from Lees Ferry. If you want just a hint of Lake Powell, consider a half-day trip into Antelope Canyon. For good reason,

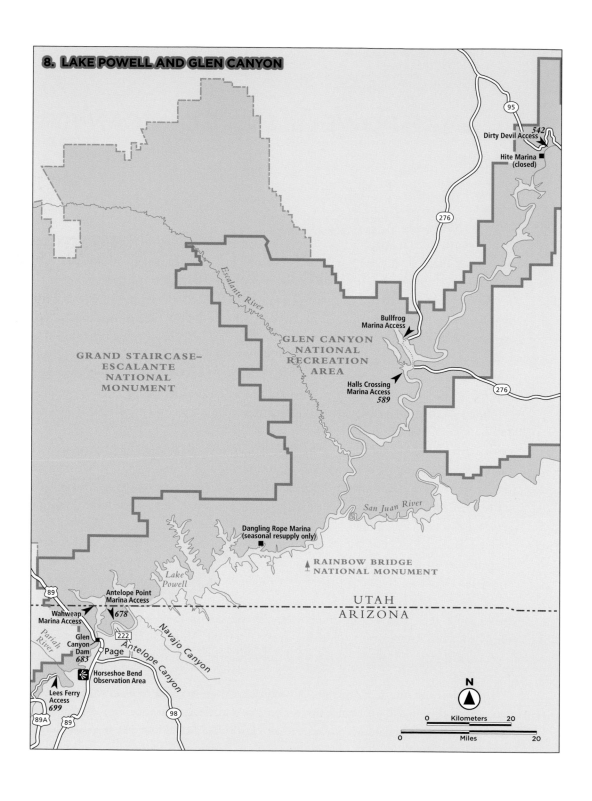

8. LAKE POWELL AND GLEN CANYON

95

542
Dirty Devil Access

Hite Marina
(closed)

276

Escalante River

Bullfrog
Marina Access

GLEN CANYON
NATIONAL
RECREATION
AREA

276

GRAND STAIRCASE–
ESCALANTE
NATIONAL
MONUMENT

Halls Crossing
Marina Access
589

San Juan River

Dangling Rope Marina
(seasonal resupply only)

▲ RAINBOW BRIDGE
NATIONAL MONUMENT

89

Lake
Powell

Antelope Point
Marina Access

UTAH
ARIZONA

Wahweap
Marina Access
678

Pariah
River

222

Glen
Canyon
Dam
683

Antelope Canyon

Navajo Canyon

Page

Horseshoe Bend
Observation Area

Lees Ferry
Access
699

89A   **89**

98

N

0   Kilometers   20

0   Miles   20

Sunrise over the desert buttes surrounding Page, AZ.

this is a popular paddling trip. During high season, early morning will have cooler temps and a quieter atmosphere. The scenery is remarkable, and at the end continues an excellent slot canyon hike. Many other trips are possible, including plenty of overnights.

Keep in mind that because the main reservoir channel is narrow and often cliff-lined, reverb waves from motor traffic form throughout the day in high-traffic areas. Also, strong up-canyon winds (from the west) are possible any time of year but are particularly pronounced during high season. For these reasons, most through-paddlers elect to cross during late fall, winter, or early spring. No matter when you go, this area is definitely worth a visit and has much to offer even if, for many river folks, it's a reminder of what was lost with the damming of Glen Canyon.

Duration: To through-paddle the entire segment, you're looking at around 10 days–2+ weeks, depending on winds, day length, and side explorations. From Dirty Devil to Hall's Crossing, about 3–6 days. From Hall's Crossing to Antelope, maybe 6–10 days.

A quiet December night on Lake Powell is captured by adventure photographer Forest Woodward. Check out his awesome short documentary, *The Important Places*, about taking his dad down the Grand Canyon.
FOREST WOODWARD

Access: The gravel boat ramp at Dirty Devil access (N37 53.29' / W110 24.04') is the farthest north/upstream access. About 50 lake miles south/downstream, there's Hall's Crossing Marina (N37 27.95' / W110 43.16') on the south shore; Bullfrog Marina (N37 30.77' / W110 43.97') is in a side channel, 3 miles to the north. Note that Dangling Rope Marina offers no vehicle access, only boat-in resupply. The next access from Hall's Crossing is 90 miles south/downstream to Antelope Marina (N36 57.95' / W111 26.53') on south shore. A final access point is Wahweap Marina (N36 59.68' / W111 29.00') in Wahweap Bay, north of the dam.

Logistics: Self-shuttles from Dirty Devil will route south of the reservoir (through Monument Valley, score!), using UT 95, UT 261, US 163, US 160, AZ 98, and connector roads. To Antelope Marina, it's 230 miles and 4 hours, one way. To Wahweap, it's a bit more mileage and 15 minutes more.

Season and weather: Year round, but late fall–early spring is quietest time for paddling. Annual precipitation is less than 7 inches, but high winds and violent thunderstorms can happen all year. Summer days are in the 90s, with nights in the 60s. Winter days are 40s and 50s, with nights in the 20s and 30s. Elevation at Page, AZ, is about 4,100'.

Water level and character: Yep, there are some real characters out there. Oh, reservoir level and projections can be found here: www.usbr.gov/uc/water/crsp/cs/gcd.html.

Challenges and safety: Up-canyon winds are common, especially in warmer months; drastic shifts in weather and sudden thunderstorms and waves possible; especially in the main channel and especially around Wahweap and Antelope, expect heavy motor traffic and reverb waves during high season. For all these reasons, consider paddling near shore.

Boats: Long boats, like sea kayaks and touring kayaks, are best for longer trips. Sit-on-tops are popular for day trips. SUPs also popular, especially for side canyon explorations, but prepare for wind and wakes in main channel.

Camping: Primitive camping is allowed throughout Glen Canyon National Recreation Area. When camping more than 200 yards from a developed area, paddlers must carry an approved portable toilet or enzyme-based waste bag system (aka poop tube).

Supplies: Page, AZ, has everything you'll need.

Regulations, agencies, fees: Glen Canyon NRA has a list of regulations on their website: www.nps.gov/glca. To access some marinas requires a vehicle entry fee or National Parks Pass.

Called the "backhaul" section, these 15 miles of flowing Colorado River are actually the remnants of Glen Canyon between the dam and Lees Ferry.

Maps: *National Geographic* Waterproof Trails Illustrated #213, Glen Canyon National Recreation Area covers almost everything. If you go into Escalante arm, there's #710, Canyons of the Escalante.

Outfitters and services: The companies below offer a variety of guided day trips, multidays, motor-supported kayaking trips to distant side canyons, and rentals. All are located in Page, AZ.

Hidden Canyon Kayak: (928) 660-1836; www.lakepowellhiddencanyonkayak.com

Kayak Lake Powell: (928) 660-0778; kayakpowell.com

Lake Powell Paddleboards & SUP: (928) 645-4017; lakepowellpaddleboards.com

In 2015, five adventurers did something many activists would consider environmental sacrilege. They visited the reservoir known as Lake Powell, paddling nearly 100 miles from Hall's Crossing to Antelope Marina over 9 days. In this chapter, two members of the group share photos and two others share their experiences below. Hilary Oliver is a writer and filmmaker whose work has appeared in *Outside*, *Adventure Journal*, *Climbing*, and more (visit hilarymoliver .com). Sinjin Eberle is communications director of the nonprofit American Rivers. Visit www.americanrivers.org to read his articles about the modern realities of Glen Canyon Dam.

Mike: So, why did you paddle there and how did it feel?

Hilary: The idea came from Sinjin. We wanted to explore the consequences of Glen Canyon Dam and use the trip to tell the larger story of water resources in the area. Initially, I had negative feelings about the dam, and those remained throughout the trip. Despite this, I was able to enjoy the beauty of the desert landscape around us. It felt otherworldly to paddle between massive sandstone buttes. But it was always tinged with the heartache of what lie beneath the water.

Mike: Can we discuss what was lost beneath the reservoir?

Hilary: If you've never seen photos of Glen Canyon before it was flooded, check out the book *Glen Canyon Before Lake Powell* by Eleanor Inskip. Picture the landscape around Moab or Arches National Park. Or Canyonlands, where the Green and Colorado Rivers flow through canyons like Labyrinth and Stillwater. Glen Canyon was full of smoothed sandstone rock formations, plus countless artifacts and ruins, all lost when the area flooded.

Mike: What was it like paddling across in December?

Hilary: Our days were short, and we covered many miles each day. Occasionally, we had headwinds, which slowed our progress. We saw very few motorboats the entire trip and usually from far away. In camp, the temperatures were chilly. We spent many hours in sleeping bags and bivy sacks, avoiding getting up to pee. We were looking for solitude, and we got it.

But we found reminders of the summer hordes at campsites, especially close to the marinas. One of the best spots I've ever camped was in a cove surrounded by sandstone walls, perched above a small beach. I'll never forget the sunrise—the red walls across the water looked like they were glowing from within. But the beach below was littered with all sorts of trash. All the living vegetation was stripped—torn to shreds by houseboaters looking for firewood. It must have been party central in the summer.

Paddling toward camp on a winter crossing of Lake Powell. For more great adventure stories and pics check out semi-rad.com! BRENDAN LEONARD

Mike: What did you learn from the trip?

Sinjin: I've known since a young age that many people want to rip down the dam, free Glen Canyon, and repair an emotional gash in the spirits of many people. I read Abbey's *Monkey Wrench Gang*; I get it. But the problem with dam removal or recent alternatives like filling Lake Mead first is the science doesn't work out. At least not yet. Plus, dam removal would have serious consequences. Economic consequences for the people that depend upon the reservoir. And major legal ramifications due to minimum water deliveries that must be made by the upper basin to the lower basin and Mexico. This could lead to new dams being built on other upper basin rivers, including the Green and Yampa.

Mike: Among conservationists, isn't advocating to keep the dam more radical than its destruction?

Sinjin: Many concerns about Glen Canyon Dam are legitimate and will eventually come true. The reservoir is unsustainable. But emotions and polarization sometimes lead to rushed exaggerations not based on evidence. Yes, the reservoir

Floating inside Cathedral in the Desert is a surreal experience. Found only on the Escalante River arm of Lake Powell, about 620 paddling miles down the Powell route. FOREST WOODWARD

is filling with sediment, but recent interpretations of sonar surveys suggest the underwater mountain of sediment will take hundreds of years to reach the dam's intake pipes—longer than the dam is designed to last. That finding came from Dr. Jack Schmidt, a watershed sciences professor at Utah State, who recently completed an in-depth study of Fill Mead First, a popular scenario for draining the reservoir.

The idea behind Fill Mead First is there are two huge reservoirs in one of the hottest, driest regions in the country. But both reservoirs are less than half full. The argument goes that collecting all the water in one pool would lead to less evaporation and seepage. Glen Canyon Dam would be left in place if needed in the future, and the water would pass around the dam through existing tunnels. Then, Glen Canyon could begin to heal. The problem is Schmidt's study concludes evaporation would be about the same. Plus, seepage concerns may be overstated. And there's no way of knowing how this might affect the Grand Canyon. The next dam relicensing won't occur until 2035. In the meantime, more scientific study is necessary to assess the true situation.

Mike: It's brave for dam skeptics to call a truce with Lake Powell and say, "Let's proceed rationally." But would you paddle there again?

Hilary: I do think the loss of Glen Canyon is a travesty. And paddling the reservoir was a real reminder of the West's dwindling water supply. During the trip, I had a serious epiphany about my own water consumption. Not eating meat has become part of my own philosophy. I feel less guilty by not contributing to the massive amount of water used to raise feed for stock animals. But whether you are cool with the dam or hate the dam, paddling there is a truly unique experience. It's a desert, and there are no natural lakes like this. I would definitely go again. I'd even add more time to explore side canyons.

Additional resources: If you're as curious as I am about the polarized and emotional debate surrounding Glen Canyon, may I suggest two things? (1) Go paddle the reservoir and visit the area to understand what's there now. (2) Take a gander at some images from before the reservoir was built to understand the perspective of dam opponents. The Glen Canyon Institute, which advocates for dam removal, curates a photo gallery: www.glencanyon.org/media_center/photos. And before anyone starts yelling about bias, just take a look first. What could it hurt?

Highlights: (***Note:*** These mileage markers are taken at center line of main channel as distance in downstream direction from Dirty Devil access.) On eastern side of the channel, Hite Marina sits high and dry like a set from a postapocalyptic TV show. • Bullfrog Marina is 3 miles north up side channel, and Halls Crossing Marina is on eastern shore at mile 46. • The Escalante Arm enters from the north, with access to Cathedral in the Desert at mile 78. • Around mile 81, Hole in the Rock, a crack in the canyon rim enlarged by Mormon settlers to lower wagons, can be found to the northeast up a side channel. • Reflection Canyon, made famous by *Nat Geo* photographer Michael Melford during low reservoir level in 2006, is found in side channel to the north near mile 88. • A side channel to the southeast, at mile 96, leads a few miles to Rainbow Bridge National Monument. • Dangling Rope Marina, with boat-in-only access, is located 1 mile up side channel to the northeast at mile 89. • Labyrinth Canyon is a popular overnight trip to the south at mile 123, typically reached from Antelope Marina. • Navajo Canyon is another popular day trip out of Antelope, found to the east at mile 131. • Antelope Marina is on the south shore at mile 136. • Antelope Canyon is to the southeast at mile 137.

PADDLING: ANTELOPE CANYON

If you're debating over Lake Powell, consider paddling one of the many side canyons. Here I draw attention to the most accessible and most popular. Just going early in the morning can often lessen the crowds.

Access: Antelope Marina boat ramp (N36 57.95' / W111 26.53').

Duration: It will take about 4–6 hours to paddle round trip. One mile to the canyon mouth, 2 miles to the back of the canyon, 6 miles round trip. Plus, there's a 2-mile hike one way up lower Antelope, if you're interested.

Boats: Any type of boat can get in there, but a kayak or SUP is the easiest for getting through the final slots at the back.

Hiking through lower Antelope Canyon can induce dizzying visuals, like a magic eye image. Below the famous (upper) Antelope slot canyon, the lower section can be reached only by paddling

PADDLING: GLEN CANYON DAM TO LEES FERRY (BACKHAUL)

If you only experience one part of this segment, then consider the backhaul section. The scenery is amazing, with sheer canyon walls rising 1,000 feet in many spots. The current is swift and clear flatwater. There are a few opportunities for side explorations. It's a world-class trout fishery. Give it a shot.

Duration: 15 miles; 4–6 hours paddling or camp overnight.

Access: Paddlers must reserve a backhaul motorboat from Lees Ferry, which carries paddlers and equipment up the river to just below Glen Canyon. Take-out is at Lees Ferry (N36 51.95' / W111 35.22'), where cars can be parked overnight.

Camping: There are about a dozen campsites, all first-come with pit toilets.

Due to the limited backhaul schedule, I've twice carried (dragged) boats in on the Ropes Trail (more like a nontechnical rappel). Read about the adventure in "A Lees Ferry to Glen Canyon Loop?", the first installment of my "Weekend Expeditions" series.
NATE HOWARD

My whole paddling career, I've heard a powerful story involving a disastrous 1950s trade in the Colorado River basin between the Bureau of Reclamation and David Brower of the Sierra Club. Basically, a proposed dam just below Echo Park on the Green River, inside Dinosaur National Monument, would not be built by BOR in exchange for a different dam being built in Glen Canyon. I first heard this story as a 19-year-old California guide, then read about it soon after in Marc Reisner's *Cadillac Desert* and other books. Later, it came up occasionally while paddling in the Ozarks and Southeast. Then, I encountered it in force as an adventure writer returning to the West to explore the Powell route, at which time I discovered this "trade" may never have happened. Let's discuss.

In the twentieth century, especially during the Bureau of Reclamation's midcentury dam-building craze, it was all the rage to build big flashy dams in some of the most scenic river canyons across the West. In 1923, the city of San Francisco built one in Yosemite National Park's Hetch Hetchy Valley, which was said to be equal in beauty to nearby Yosemite Valley. Eventually, after the Colorado River Compact was signed in 1922, plans were drawn up for the Colorado River

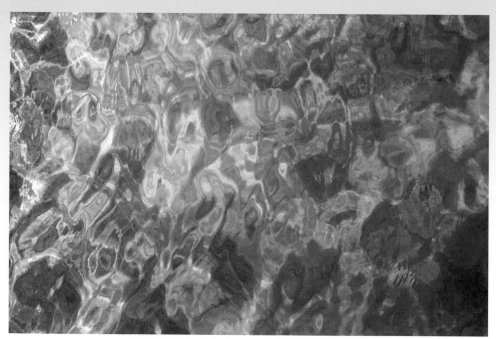

There's no pretending the water at Lake Powell isn't beautiful. Angry critics will point out that it's unnatural, and defensive adherents will respond, "Who cares?" Powell pilgrims swim lightly; there is partisanship on all sides.

Storage Project (CRSP). At various times, BOR considered many more dam sites across the Colorado River basin than were eventually used. And plenty of these unused dam sites, often involving exploratory drilling, fall along the Powell route and can be visited today.

A dam was considered in Lower Granite Gorge of the Grand Canyon, at Bridge Canyon, about 934 miles down the route, or 235 miles from Lees Ferry. Prior to the CRSP, a dam was also considered at two spots in Marble Canyon, 32 and 40 miles down from Lees Ferry. The site was so remote, it required building a 3,400-foot cable tram. The project was eventually abandoned, maybe because no one really wanted to carry a billion bags of concrete down a cable tram to flood one of the coolest canyons on earth? A dam was considered in Gray Canyon, near Coal Creek, about 350 miles down the route, which would have flooded the Green River into the heart of Deso.

And two dams were proposed in Dinosaur National Monument. One was an afterbay dam at Split Mountain, not far from the boat ramp, which would have flooded Split Mountain and Whirlpool Canyons, all the way to the foot of the most controversial site of all. The Echo Park Dam site is about a mile into Whirlpool Canyon, around 155 miles down the route. Basically, if not for public opposition, every major canyon on the Powell route might have become a long chain of less-than-half-full reservoirs.

Enter David Brower, a decorated lieutenant in the 10th Mountain Division, who returned from World War II to his job at the University of California Press, in Berkeley, coincidentally just a few miles from where I grew up. Brower became involved with the Sierra Club—a hiking group that evolved into an environmental advocacy organization—eventually becoming its first executive director. When the CRSP plans were being developed in the 1950s, Brower opposed the dam in Echo Park on the grounds that no new dams should be built in national parks or monuments, which were supposed to preserve these natural, cultural, and historic spaces for recreation and study. Brower saw Echo as another Hetch Hetchy, which had required an act of Congress to bypass the conservation status of Yosemite National Park.

In short, through the advocacy of Brower and the Sierra Club, public opposition to the Echo Park Dam led the BOR to cancel plans for its construction. And this decision set a precedent for successful oppositions to other dams in national parks and monuments, such as Bridge Canyon. But, to get Echo Park excluded, it's alleged that Brower made a compromise, agreeing not to oppose Glen Canyon Dam, which was located in an empty desert that few were familiar with.

Well, once I began exploring the Flaming Gorge area, I began to encounter outright contradictions to this claim. The counter story was that there was no trade, that when Echo Park Dam was canceled, Flaming Gorge Dam was instead moved forward to replace the loss in anticipated storage. While there were people advocating to stop Glen Canyon, these were smaller and less-organized groups whose collective voices were much quieter when compared to the broader-reaching Sierra Club. Brower's argument was certainly logical, opposing dams on the basis of being inside national parks or monuments. This counter story alleges that Brower only later learned about the remarkable beauty, ecological diversity, and cultural significance of Glen Canyon by taking a river trip there before the reservoir filled. And Brower felt terribly guilty that he hadn't done anything to save Glen Canyon.

As I explored the Powell route, I began inquiring about this "trade." When I asked, most folks repeated the story as a trade of one dam for another. Brower traded Glen Canyon away to the BOR for Echo Park and later regretted the decision, like an exchange of baseball cards that could be seen from space. But when I asked about the discrepancy, many agreed that a group of hikers from Berkeley probably wasn't spending hours in smoky room negotiations with a powerful government agency. It just doesn't add up. When I tried to trace down any primary source material, the best I could find was a foreword Brower wrote for *The Place No One Knew*.

In *Cadillac Desert*, Marc Reisner mentions a compromise to leave Glen Canyon Dam alone. And Reisner cites an earlier edition, which I've never read, of *The Place No One Knew*, quoting Brower this way: "'Glen Canyon died in 1963. . . . I was partly responsible for its needless death. So were you. Neither you nor I, nor anyone else, knew it well enough to insist that at all costs it should endure.'" Reisner continues, by adding a key point: "Never again, Brower vowed, was he going to *compromise* over such a dam." [Those italics are *all* mine.]

Well, in the 2000 edition of *The Place No One Knew*, Brower's story has changed somewhat. He writes, "Glen Canyon Dam would not have been built if I hadn't let a war be lost. Between 1950 and 1956 I switched from advocating a higher Glen Canyon Dam to insisting that there be no dam at all, but I was directed by the Sierra Club's executive committee to end my opposition to that mistake, and for no explicable reason I obeyed. But let's not wait years or generations to correct the mistake and drain Lake Powell."

Okay, that's pretty different. And the two different lessons, from these two vastly different stories Brower told many years apart, seem particularly significant for understanding how water resource discussions in the West have stagnated, as pointed out by contributor Tom Minckley on page 130. Glen Canyon Dam has long been considered a problematic dam, and the problems seem to relate to its builders blindly moving forward despite key gaps in knowledge at key times.

Glen Canyon was designed using Hoover as a template, but Hoover was built in solid granite, while Glen Canyon is built in Navajo sandstone, which creates dramatic and sheer cliffs but does so through flaking off from weathering. Filling the dam is rare, as it was proposed using inflated precipitation estimates taken from a period of abnormally wet years. And the one time they did manage to fill it, the overexuberant operators forgot to plan for potential spring flooding. Then, in 1983, the dam nearly collapsed when the Navajo sandstone in the spillways began flaking away.

Had Glen Canyon not been turned into a reservoir and National Recreation Area, it probably would have still become a National Monument or Park. Given the financial boom from tourism in nearby places like Zion and Bryce, it's just as likely a tourist-based economy would have arisen like at Grand Canyon, and one that was not dependent on reservoir levels. But now that the dam and reservoir are there, it can't just be yanked out or bypassed based on regret and anger.

The view from the Carl Hayden Visitor Center at Glen Canyon Dam near Page, Arizona.

What would happen to all the industries, communities, and people, upstream and downstream, who rely upon the dam?

And that's the disturbing message of a trade that never happened. Brower's message in his first foreword seems more likely. Glen Canyon was a major boondoggle that happened because of a lack of knowledge. But his second message in 2000 has shifted to blaming the very idea of compromise, an attitude which likely shuts down discussion and creates polarized entrenchment. Suddenly, Brower always knew what was best, but in the 1950s, he just didn't stick to his guns by holding his position, and a war was lost. His call to action seems to be a rush back into battle by destroying the dam. But the problems created by the dam can't be fixed by blindly repeating the mistakes of its creators. To move forward, it seems, a new and more knowledgeable approach will be needed. And a good first step might be going to Lake Powell and seeing what's there. I suggest taking a paddle.

Lake Powell kayaking guide Nate Howard paddles at river level through Horseshoe Bend on his first trip down the Colorado River.

Outfitters and services: In 2018, Wilderness River Adventures became the sole provider of commercial backhaul operations for rafters and kayakers; (800) 992-8022; www.riveradventures.com.

In some circumstances, authorized fishing guides are able to backhaul kayakers and boats, and a list is available here: www.nps.gov/glca/learn/management/guidedservices .htm.

Highlights: About 6 miles below the dam, there are petroglyphs on river-left at Ferry Swale campsite. • Paddling through Horseshoe Bend. • Camping anywhere, including at "Nine" Mile Campsites below the famous lookout, about 7 miles down. • Waterhole Canyon enters on river-left at mile 12, offering side exploration.

1869, PART V: IS GLEN CANYON MORE LIGHT AND AIRY THAN OUR BOATS?

Okay, who ate all the half-starved coyote? • let's not settle for "Mound Canyon" • does it always rain in the desert? • off the map at Little Colorado River

As the nine men passed below the Dirty Devil, a break in the canyons provided a glimpse of what would be later called the Henry Mountains. Named by Almon Harris Thompson, lead surveyor on the second expedition, this would be the final U.S. mountain range named by white Americans. Bradley thought the mountains seemed of harder rock than any previously seen on the expedition. He pondered the basalts and granites, which explorers of the lower Colorado River had predicted would fill the unknown Grand Canyon.

Meanwhile, this newest canyon began with low walls and bluffs upon which the men stopped to inspect the ruins of a home built by what today are called Ancestral Puebloans. Rowing into strong headwinds, common throughout the area, the group reached the mouth of the San Juan River around July 31. About a half mile up a nearby side canyon, Powell and men discovered a dazzling alcove worn into the sandstone. A hundred yards long, 50 yards wide, with an overhanging ceiling of smooth rock offering just a narrow skylight, perhaps 25 feet across. At the bottom was a small lake and enough room for 2,000 people, according to Sumner. Filling it with the 1830s' song "Old House at Home," they called it Music Temple. Completely flooded behind the rising waters of the controversial Glen Canyon Dam, the temple was supposedly similar to the now half-flooded Cathedral in the Desert, which can be visited by paddlers today. It's likely Walter Powell crooned the lyrics:

"Oh! the old house at home where my forefathers dwelt / Where a child at the feet of my mother I knelt / Where she taught me the pray'r, where she read me the page / Which, if infancy lisps, is the solace of age / My heart, 'mid all changes, wherever I roam / Ne'er loses its love for the old house at home!"

Bradley was more preoccupied by the rations situation. The men had seen three sheep that morning but caught none. They were down to 15 pounds of bacon and short on everything except flour, coffee, and dried apples—a selection that would make even a modern rafter on an all-smoothie diet cringe. Two days before, Dunn had killed a half-starved coyote, the only animal taken for a week. Then, on August 2, Sumner killed one sheep but lost a second, securing 80 pounds of fresh meat, part of which was dried. While they didn't know it, this would be the last large animal harvested on the expedition.

The men pushed onward into this deepening and diverse canyon, which was formed from smoothed sandstone. Sometimes they passed rock domes, which caused the coining of Mound Canyon. In other places, monuments towered over the river, so it became

Glen Canyon as photographed by
James Fennemore in 1872.
US Geological Survey

Monument Canyon. In side canyons, beautiful glens and alcoves stretched back from the river, so Powell landed on Glen Canyon. Sheer walls rose above for miles before subsiding upstream from the mouth of the Paria River, a spot that within a few years would become Lees Ferry. However, on this fourth day in August, the men—over 700 miles and 72 days down from Green River Station—were unsure of their location. Hungry, stressed, and exhausted, they believed themselves to be passing the Crossing of the Fathers, located about 35 miles upstream. There, in 1776, the similarly struggling Dominguez-Escalante land expedition was guided by local Native Americans to ford the river.

Down into a new canyon they went, one which dropped inside a plateau, like a deepening crack in a level floor. Traveling beneath sheer walls of polished limestone, Powell would decide the rocks looked like marbles of cream, pink, purple, brown, and red. As before, some rapids were run while others were portaged. On one such portage, they gouged a hole in *Maid of the Cañon*, necessitating a layover camp for repairs. Bradley remarked the "constant banging on rocks has begun to tell sadly on them and they are growing old faster, if possible, than we are."

It began raining, so tents were built for the first time in over a month, since their layover in the Uinta Basin. Now, the Colorado River turned namesake red and was rising. While the men worked in camp, Powell and brother Walter climbed up the cliffs on river-right, collecting fossils and seeking high ground to observe the August 7 eclipse. But the storm clouds were thick, and the observation failed. They descended as night arrived. Rain fell in torrents, and the path was obscured. Without shelter, they hunkered down on the cliffs and waited out the storm until morning.

Continuing downriver, Bradley noted they'd never made so many portages in one day—they'd never had so little gear and rations to carry. Their clothes were ragged. For months, the standard river dress was long underwear and shirts, but these had shredded until barely keeping them decent. Over the coming days, the men's experiences aligned closely with a modern Grand Canyon trip, scanty dress included—carrying boats and everlasting hunger emphatically excepted.

One morning, Powell walked for a mile atop a pavement of polished limestone. Around lunchtime, they scrambled up a side canyon through shimmering pools of water. They passed sheer walls of banded rock and stared up at Vasey's Paradise, a spring that gushes from a cliff face and tumbles as a waterfall through 50 feet of mossy oasis. Bradley called it the prettiest sight of the whole trip. Sumner found it beautiful, but his notes discourage anyone from trying to hike in to see it—with steep canyon walls rising several thousand feet.

Around noon on August 10, Powell had a realization. Given the river's course south, their current southern latitude, and the steeper gradient in Marble Canyon, he concluded they'd already passed the Paria. Soon they would reach the Chiquito, or Little Colorado River. Two hours later, according to Bradley, they arrived. From the rains,

A portrait of John Steward taken by
J. K. Hillers in Glen Canyon in 1872.
US GEOLOGICAL SURVEY

the LCR was running muddy brown, and there were signs of past Native American habitation along its banks. They laid over for a few days to determine lat/long and fix this major blank spot on US maps. The men were not pleased by this delay, but Bradley believed them willing to do what was needed for a successful expedition.

Meanwhile, discussions of James White circled among the men. He controversially claimed to have floated through the entire Grand Canyon on a hastily built log raft. Arriving at the mouth of the Virgin River, a bit closer to death than civilization, he said he came down it all in 11 days. Bradley wished White's story was true, as this would suggest an easy passage for the expedition. But Bradley, Powell, and Sumner all doubted the tale. And with good reason—theirs would not be an easy passage.

The 1869 adventure continues on page 191 . . .

Marble Canyon, near the Little Colorado River, is captured by J. K. Hillers in 1872.
US GEOLOGICAL SURVEY

GRAND CANYON

WHAT IS THERE TO SAY ABOUT THE GRAND CANYON that hasn't been said thousands of times before? Used up all the damn adjectives, mutter, mutter. . . . Instead, how about a few less-than-stellar quotes by cranky visitors to the south rim taken from some infamous review websites. "Not much going on and real big." " . . . No animals, no greenery, no clear blue streams . . . just a muddy river, rock, and sheer cliffs. You'll go 'ooh' and 'ahh' for 30 seconds and then feel guilty that you're ready to leave . . ." "I've seen grander."

I'm definitely cherry picking, because most comments by visitors to the rim, typically the south, tend to be much more positive—often downright ecstatic. Many describe the visit as awe-inspiring, breath-taking, or overwhelming. It's that last point—overwhelming—that seems most relevant to understanding why viewing the Grand Canyon from the rim can be a challenge for certain adventurous people who prefer more active experiences. At other national parks, such visitors might arrive by car inside a canyon, like Zion or Yosemite, and the experience begins the moment they step outside and start walking beneath the drama. Or take Bryce, another rim-based park, where the prime attraction is a thousand hoodoos a thousand feet away that you can almost reach over and touch.

At the Grand Canyon—other than the distant geology, which also takes concentrated effort to decipher—the prime attraction is the vastness and emptiness. It's practically the absence of tangible experience. For that reason, many of those ecstatic visitors to the rim overcome the distance with day hikes partway down, or they use telescopes, binoculars, and visitor guides to help view the attraction from afar. But that's not enough for everyone. It wasn't for me at 19 when I arrived for the first time to the rim and felt, honestly, underwhelmed.

It wasn't until I backpacked down into the canyon for a week—not until my legs and shoulders ached, my hands brushed against basement rocks, I swam in the river, and leaned at a 45-degree angle into the winds on Horseshoe Plateau—that the canyon felt real to me. When I came back up to the rim 8 days later, I felt like I could see things better from afar. And so, every time I'm lucky enough to run the river through

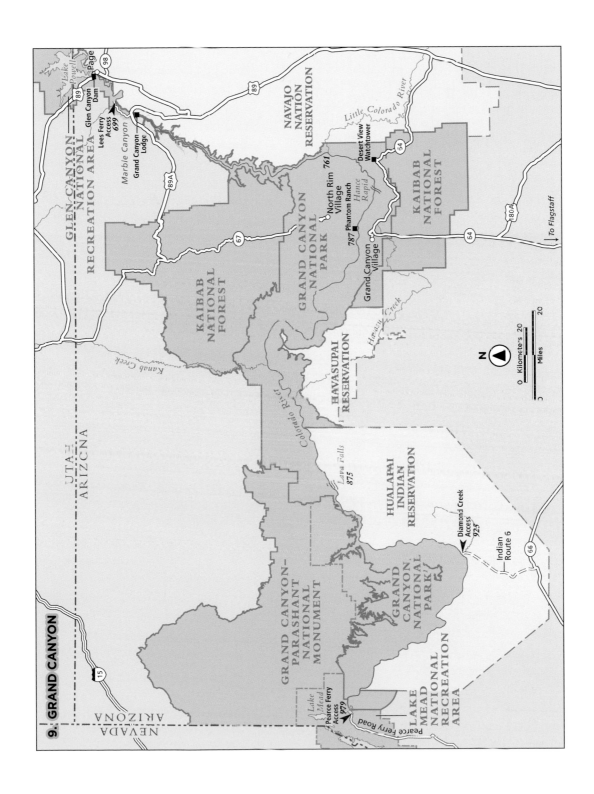

9. GRAND CANYON

UTAH
ARIZONA

NEVADA
ARIZONA

15

Lake Powell

Page
98

Glen Canyon Dam

89

Lees Ferry
Access
699

GLEN CANYON
NATIONAL
RECREATION AREA

Marble Canyon

Grand Canyon Lodge

89A

Kanab Creek

89

NAVAJO NATION
RESERVATION

Little Colorado River

Desert View
Watchtower

64

North Rim
Village

761

67

KAIBAB
NATIONAL
FOREST

GRAND CANYON
NATIONAL PARK

Hance Rapid

787 Phantom Ranch

Grand Canyon Village

KAIBAB
NATIONAL
FOREST

64

180A

To Flagstaff

Havasu Creek

HAVASUPAI
RESERVATION

Colorado River

Lava Falls
875

HUALAPAI
INDIAN
RESERVATION

Diamond Creek
Access
925

Indian
Route 6

66

GRAND CANYON–
PARASHANT NATIONAL
MONUMENT

Lake Mead

Pearce Ferry
Access
979

Pearce Ferry Road

GRAND
CANYON
NATIONAL
PARK

LAKE
MEAD
NATIONAL
RECREATION
AREA

LAKE MEAD
NATIONAL RECREATION
AREA

N

0 Kilometers 20

0 Miles 20

"YOU CANNOT SEE THE GRAND CANYON IN ONE VIEW, AS IF IT WERE A CHANGELESS SPECTACLE FROM WHICH A CURTAIN MIGHT BE LIFTED, BUT TO SEE IT YOU HAVE TO TOIL FROM MONTH TO MONTH THROUGH ITS LABYRINTHS."

—*John Wesley Powell*

Grand Canyon, I pair it with a return visit to the rim. Each time I do this, my perspective of the canyon changes. The view from the rim seems more tangible, less overwhelming, and a lot more engaging.

A river trip through Grand Canyon—whether a few days by motor rig, a week or two by kayak, or a month-long expedition by raft—forces the

"The cañon has lofty walls, much of the way perpendicular, and wherever the rocks have fallen in or there is a side cañon we have a rapid." —George Bradley, boatman on the first expedition @PeterHolcombe

A lone figure stands on a cliff near Toroweap overlook in the Grand Canyon. That could be you. Check out more awesome images at www.amysmartinphotography.com! AMY MARTIN

visitor to intimately confront the particulars of the Grand Canyon. Drop a foot or an oar into the river. Feel the spray from collapsing waves on your face. Scramble up from shore into side canyons where you can touch both walls at once. Hike to ancestral native ruins. Swim underneath waterfalls in clear side streams. Watch bighorn sheep trot along an improbable ledge. Count greenery in the form of blooming yuccas and barrel cacti. Sit back in a camp chair and read about things like the Nankoweap Granaries or lava dams created by eruptions from the Uinkaret volcanic field. And, as darkness settles, watch stars hover between rocky cliffs while listening to the river rush past.

Doesn't get much grander than that, which is why descending the Colorado River through Grand Canyon became the *trip of a lifetime*. The more effort you put in, the more the canyon will reveal itself in unforgettable ways. How's your schedule looking a few years out?

"The limestone of this canyon is often polished, and makes a beautiful marble. Sometimes the rocks are of many colors— white, gray, pink, and purple, with saffron hints. It is with very great labor that we make progress . . ." —John Wesley Powell

Duration: This is complicated. The classic private trip is 226 or 281 miles, but some participants can join or leave trips at Phantom Ranch, using Bright Angel Trail. NPS sets maximum trip durations depending on the season (otherwise plenty o' dirtbags would live down there). Many groups choose the maximum duration allowed. In summer, this is 16 days for Lees Ferry to Diamond Creek, plus a few more days to reach Pearce. In winter, it's 25 days to Diamond, though it can certainly be faster, with many boaters finding about 21 days to be a great winter or shoulder season length. In recent years, self-support kayak trips have been quickening the pace and even setting speed records. Commercial trips, some of which use motors and helicopter access at Whitmore Wash, offer many more durations, from 4 days to 2 weeks. Some commercial companies run kayak support trips; see outfitters list for details.

Access: Start at Lees Ferry (N36 W51.95' / N111 35.22'); optional passenger exchange at Phantom Ranch (N36 6.00' / W112 5.59'); end at Diamond Creek (N35 45.96' / W113 22.39') or Pearce Ferry (N36 7.54' / W113 58.94').

Logistics: Most groups hire a shuttle service or use a multiservice private outfitter, offering equipment rentals, meal packing, shuttles, and more (see list below). A self-shuttle from Lees Ferry to Diamond Creek, using US 89, I-40, AZ 66, and connector roads, is 260 miles and 4.5 hours each way. To Pearce Ferry, using US 89, I-40, US 93, and Pearce Ferry Road, is 360 miles and 5.5 hours each way.

Season and weather: Year round! (Got weather year round, too.) It's important to remember that the river level in the inner canyon is 5,000 feet below the rim. Approximate elevations are Lees Ferry at 3,100', Phantom Ranch at 2,450', and Diamond Creek at 1,400'. Thus, temperatures in winter are cold but manageable, though most groups consider drysuits a necessity; snow rarely reaches the canyon floor. Shoulder season is quite mild. Summer is a scorcher, like throw buckets of water on the sand before stepping onshore; daytime highs often exceed 100°F. Monsoon season runs from mid-June through mid-Sept, making afternoon thunderstorms possible.

Water level and character: Class IV—and let the debate begin! The Grand Canyon uses an . . . interesting . . . system in which rapids are rated from 1 to 10, with 10 typically being compared to class V. Among many boaters, the Grand Canyon is famous for overstating the rating of their rapids, and for good reason. Frankly, most rapids are class II–III—but the volume is higher, typically around 10,000 cfs, which means the water moves swiftly. About a dozen rapids are rated as class V, but they're more class IV–IV+ in difficulty—due to consequences, they are often rated as class V because of the remote and inaccessible nature of the canyon. If someone swims a rapid and is bruised or breaks a bone, you can't just call it a day and go home. Thus, every rapid tends to carry slightly higher consequences. At high water, maybe over 25,000

Plenty of scrambling opportunities in Matkatamiba Canyon, aka "Matkat," a favorite stop, about 848 paddling miles down the route. WHIT RICHARDSON

COMMERCIAL TRIPS THROUGH GRAND CANYON

Below is a list of commercial outfitters offering guided trips by oar raft or motor rig. Many outfitters offer specialty trips that emphasize hiking, geology, astronomy, archeology, music, art, or photography. Custom options may include paddleboats, inflatable kayaks, hard-shell kayaking, charter trips, and accommodations for the disabled.

Many trip durations are available on various sections. Full canyon trips are typically from Lees Ferry to Pearce Ferry. Upper canyon trips are typically from Lees Ferry to Phantom Ranch. Lower canyon trips run from Phantom to Whitmore Wash, Diamond Creek, or Pearce. There are even some *lower* lower canyon trips from Whitmore or Diamond Down.

Remember that most spots on canyon trips are reserved 1 to 2 years in advance, though cancellations and openings do occur. Visit company websites for more information.

OAR TRIPS ONLY

Canyon Explorations: 6- to 17-day raft and kayak support trips; www.canyonx .com

OARS: 6- to 17-day raft and dory trips; www.oars.com

Outdoors Unlimited: 5- to 15-day raft trips; www.outdoorsunlimited.com

OAR AND MOTOR TRIPS

Arizona Raft Adventures: 6- to 16-day raft, motor, dory, and kayak support trips; azraft.com

Arizona River Runners: 3- to 13-day raft and motor trips; raftarizona.com

Canyoneers: 3- to 14-day raft and motor trips; canyoneers.com

Colorado River & Trail Expeditions: 3- to 14-day raft and motor trips; www.crate inc.com

Grand Canyon Expeditions: 8- to 16-day dory and motor trips; www.gcex.com

Grand Canyon Whitewater: 4- to 13-day raft and motor trips; www.grandcanyon whitewater.com

Hatch River Expeditions: 4- to 12-day raft and motor trips; www.hatchriver expeditions.com

Tour West: 4- to 13-day raft and motor trips; www.twriver.com

Wilderness River Adventures: 4- to 14-day raft and motor trips; www.river adventures.com

COMMERCIAL MOTOR TRIPS ONLY

Hualapai River Runners: 1- to 2-day motor trips; www.grandcanyonwest.com/ hualapai-river-runners-and-colorado-river.htm

Western River Expeditions: 3- to 7-day j-rig trips; www.westernriver.com

After your Grand Canyon trip, be prepared for many passionate debates about which camps were your favorites. @PeterHolcombe

or 30,000, the harder rapids become more difficult, which is just how rapids typically work. None of this means the canyon should be taken lightly. Competent class IV boaters have all the skills necessary to descend the canyon—and they still frequently have trouble with the rapids—that's whitewater. Gradient is roughly 8 fpm. For water levels, use guage USGS Colorado River at Lees Ferry, AZ.

Challenges and safety: Plenty. The two biggest challenges seem to relate to the greatest contradiction within the Grand Canyon: It's a remote wilderness with limited access that's subject to the pervasive and unnatural effects of Glen Canyon Dam. To the latter issue, the water is ridiculously cold. It exits the dam at 46°F and doesn't warm up much as it moves downstream—even in summer. That means hypothermia becomes a real issue for swimmers from upset boats. In cold and cooler weather, the answer is significant layering and outerwear (see page xxxv). In summer, it's trickier because the air is so hot, but you must dress for the swim. And once in the water, the rule is to get out fast but safely by swimming to a nearby boat or shore. The next issue is tides from constantly changing releases from Glen Canyon Dam. Each day there is typically a low release in the early morning hours and a higher release sometime during the day and into the evening or night. Of course, as you move downstream, this diurnal cycle has increasing lag time, which means the tides come at increasingly later times, roughly 1 hour per 5 miles, but it's a surging and ebbing river, not a rocket calculation. Always tie up rafts and pull kayaks well above the high-water line. Tie up rafts in spots where the beaches drop steeply away, otherwise, when the tide drops, the raft will sit high and dry, which could be impossible to move without large groups and even fully unloading. And remember that the release schedule can change without warning, meaning tracking the tides as you move downstream alone cannot guarantee avoiding tidal issues. Finally, because of the remote nature, everything is amplified. An untreated cut that becomes infected could lead to a necessary helicopter evacuation. Forgotten or lost medication can't be replaced. NPS provides detailed safety and evacuation guidelines in the handbook, so be sure to review these!

Boats: Pretty much any whitewater boat that can safely navigate class IV rapids will work here; NPS has a few guidelines in the handbook mentioned above.

Camping: There are many campsites established by river runners and private companies. These are named and well mapped in the topographic river guides I list below.

Supplies: Most river runners bring in supplies from afar, while others stock up in Flagstaff, AZ, which is where most private outfitters are based. Page, AZ, is the closest option to put-in for last-minute oh-crap supplies. Marble Lodge has a small store and a good restaurant for a pretrip meal, plus lodgings.

Regulations, agencies, fees: Uh, yeah. Big yeah. Grand Canyon National Park provides everything for private river runners in an excellent 33-page handbook, *Noncommercial River Trip Regulations*, available for download on their website at www.nps.gov/grca. A few items to emphasize: Private river runners are allowed to participate in only one trip per calendar year; each trip is required to have a qualified boat operator, who has experience on at least one river considered similar by NPS; Diamond Creek Road is on the Hualapai Reservation, which maintains the road and requires an access fee, with contact information available in the NPS handbook; note that most private outfitters/shuttle companies offer to arrange Hualapai fees as part of their service.

Lottery and permit: This is the hardest permit to obtain along the Powell route; private river runners must submit an application to the NPS weighted lottery via their online system at grcariverpermits.nps.gov. A great feature of the weighted lottery is that it increases the odds of winning for those applicants who have never been on a trip and those who have not been on a trip within the past 5 years. Also available

Why wouldn't you celebrate down here?

PRIVATE TRIP EQUIPMENT OUTFITTERS AND SHUTTLE SERVICES

Because of the sheer scope of planning and executing a Grand Canyon private trip, many groups arrange for assistance from a private outfitter or shuttle service. Some of these outfitters offer full services and packages, while others focus on particular offerings. Services include raft, kayak, SUP, and equipment rentals, menu planning, food purchase and packing, vehicle storage, shuttle services or drivers, and more. These companies have extensive experience with canyon logistics, so if you seek assistance with a particular situation, chances are they have a solution.

FULL-SERVICE PRIVATE OUTFITTERS WITH SHUTTLE SERVICES

Canyon R.E.O., Flagstaff, AZ: (800) 637-4604; www.canyonreo.com

Ceiba Adventures, Inc., Flagstaff, AZ: (800) 217-1060; ceibaadventures.com

Moenkopi Riverworks, Flagstaff, AZ: (928) 526-6622; www.moenkopiriverworks.com

Professional River Outfitters, Inc., Flagstaff, AZ: (800) 648-3236; www.proriver.com

DRYSUIT RENTALS

Pacific River Supply (can ship by mail), El Sobrante, CA: (510) 223-3675; pacificriversupply.com

SHUTTLE SERVICES

River Runners Shuttle Service, Meadview, AZ: (928) 564-2194; www.rrshuttleservice.com

through the lottery webpages is a 22-page handbook titled *River and Weighted Lottery Frequently Asked Questions*, which details the process and includes information on which times of year are more in demand and so forth. Look, at this point, you're probably wondering if you can get graduate-level course credit for planning a Grand Canyon trip. Honestly, that's fair. I'll look into it and see what I can do.

Maps and guides: There are many great options for topographic river maps and guides for this segment, and many river trips often carry them all, distributed across various boats. The first three include excellent sections on geology, history, and nature: *Belknap's Waterproof Grand Canyon River Guide*; *RiverMaps Guide to the Colorado River in the Grand Canyon: Lees Ferry to South Cove* by Tom Martin; *The Colorado River in*

Snow is visible on the rim during a winter hike. Watch out for barrel cactuses , which in addition to being prickly, will sometimes follow unsuspecting hikers.

Grand Canyon: River Map & Guide by Larry Stevens; *National Geographic* Waterproof Trails Illustrated Maps #263 Grand Canyon West & #262 Grand Canyon East.

Additional resources: Well! There are too many to list, but most are available at grandcanyon.org. One book I recommend, for GC trip members that enjoy hiking, is Tom Martin's *Day Hikes from the River: A Guide to 100 Hikes from Camps on the Colorado River in Grand Canyon National Park*. Fair warning, not everyone is blessed with the hiking prowess of the author, who has been described to me as half mountain goat. Luckily, there's a great range of hikes from very easy to very hard.

Highlights: Well, this is awkward. It's kind of ALL highlights. Hmm . . . Many paddlers don't realize the first 60 miles are actually through Marble Canyon, which is narrower and more confined by sheer walls than Grand Canyon proper. The current in Marble is a bit slower, with fewer and smaller rapids, compared to the famous ones downstream, except for a few spots like Soap Creek, House Rock, and the slap-happy Roaring 20s • Vasey's Paradise and Redwall Cavern, eroded into the remarkable

Redwall limestone at about mile 32, are major highlights for many • Just before mile 33 and again before mile 40 are the 1951 test bores for the proposed Marble Canyon Dam site, a sobering reminder that much of this amazing canyon might have become a reservoir • The Nankoweap Granaries are a must hike at mile 53 • The Little Colorado River enters on river-left near mile 62 and runs turquoise blue when low • The story of Crash Canyon, at mile 63, where the wreckage fell from two jetliners colliding midair, makes for gripping history • The Unkar Delta around mile 72 is worth exploring • Hance Rapid—at mile 77 and not quite 700 miles down the Powell route—marks the start of the major rapids and nearby entry to upper Granite Gorge, all a big reason why a good topo river map is needed. Phantom Ranch is a fun stop at mile 88 • Elves Chasm is an amazing waterfall pocket on river-left at mile 117 • Tapeats Creek near mile 134 is a popular and scenic side hike to Thunder River • Near mile 135, the river enters Granite Narrows, the narrowest spot in the inner gorge, where the canyon walls are only 76 feet apart • Deer Creek plummets from the right wall at mile 137. Kanab Creek, where the second expedition hiked out in 1872, is on river-right at mile 144 • "Matkat" Canyon, near mile 148, is a fun scramble through smoothed bedrock. (At this point, the paragraph is feeling fairly rhetorical, huh?) • Havasu Creek enters river-left at mile 157—just google it. Vulcan's Anvil, a midriver volcanic rock at mile 178 signals the arrival at Lava Falls at mile 179.5, the final major rapid for most trips • Whitmore Wash has a helipad where many commercial guests depart the canyon • Pumpkin Spring, at mile 213, is worth a stop • Diamond Peak becomes visible downriver above Diamond Creek, at mile 226, where most private trips stop • Powell pilgrims may enjoy continuing below, where Separation Rapids and commemorative plaque is found at mile 240 • The site of proposed Bridge Canyon Dam, in Lower Granite Gorge at mile 235, would have flooded the canyon back to Kanab Creek • I hope the point of why damming this canyon is a terrible idea has been made, so I'm going to sign off here. But FYI, there's way more than I've listed, plus more cool stuff continues all the way to Lake Mead.

PADDLING: "DIAMOND DOWN"—DIAMOND CREEK TO PEARCE FERRY

Many don't realize that the final 52 miles of the Grand Canyon—less than 15 miles of river and the rest across reservoir, depending on the storage level of Lake Mead—can be visited as a stand-alone trip. NPS allows two launches per day from Diamond Creek, which will require paying Hualapai access fees (details above). The trip will take you through Lower Granite Gorge, past the flooded site of Separation Rapids, and out from the dramatic Grand Wash Cliffs. You'll also experience frequent helicopter traffic that some river runners compare to the film *Apocalypse Now*. Perhaps not worth a stand-alone trip for most river runners, who sometimes add this on to a full canyon trip. To cross the reservoir, some groups stow a motor or bring one in at Diamond Creek, while other groups float out during the night when winds typically (hopefully) dissipate. If your time is limited or you can only do the canyon in stages, Diamond Down as a stand-alone trip may be worth considering; www.nps.gov/grca/planyourvisit/overview-diamond-ck.htm.

1869, PART VI: ABOUT THAT WHOLE "WORST RAPID" THING ABOVE GRAND CANYON

Wildest days yet • rainiest weather imaginable • biggest rapid in history • a somber moment at Separation • guess things can get worse.

As the layover at the Little Colorado stretched into a third day, Bradley noticed that Powell seemed content with sour biscuits and dried apples as long as he was taking measurements and observing geology. But the men were becoming anxious and discontent. Finally, on the morning of August 13, they pushed off into the Grand Canyon—the *great unknown*, as Powell later called it. That evening they camped above what would be called Hance Rapids, at half a mile the longest yet encountered. The men stared at the rapids, finally deciding against James White's claims to have tied himself to a log raft and floated through years before.

The next day was the wildest yet of the whole trip. After lining down the left side of Hance, they soon entered what today is called Upper Granite Gorge, a shadowy chasm of black Vishnu schist and pink Zoroaster granite. Finding a steep set of waves constricted between cliffs, with no option for portage, the men were forced to run what became Sockdolager Rapid. Powell noted, "Must run it or abandon the enterprise. Good luck!" The boats shipped plenty of water, but all came through upright. A third rapid, today called Grapevine, was reached that evening. The men clung to holds in the granite bordering the rapids as they lined boats down along the cliffs. They ate dinner in a cave and slept on a ledge where, if someone rolled, Bradley feared they might take a swim.

The next day, they reached the present location of Phantom Ranch. Powell called the stream Silver Creek but later renamed it Bright Angel, perhaps to contrast the name Dirty Devil at the head of Glen Canyon, which may have offended some of the men. Oramel discovered he'd lost the notes and map made since the Little Colorado. He went fishing in the creek but was skunked. The men spread the rations to dry and worked to make oars from found timber, when a boat suddenly shifted in the eddy. The bowline swung across and knocked the baking powder into the river, an incident that has been curiously relocated to Gray Canyon on the Green River in later years. Henceforth, the men would eat unleavened flatbread, or as modern boaters say, "Tortillas for lunch again, yay."

Sockdolager Rapid as seen by the second expedition in 1872. US Geological Survey

The weather alternated between periods of intense heat and dramatic downpours. This frequent rain had persisted, on and off, night and day, for a week now. The men were puzzled, given the harsh desert canyon surrounding them. Unwittingly, they had arrived at Grand Canyon during peak monsoon season. One evening, they witnessed a terrible thundershower, described by Bradley, the lone crew member whose notes remained detailed and thorough during increased challenges. As lightning danced and thunder echoed through the canyon, the men tied up the boats and sought shelter behind boulders. Depressions in the cliffs became thousands of silvery waterfalls and cascades, some of which turned to vapor in the warm air above the rocks and muddy river.

Days were a constant struggle with portages, long rows through flatwater, and frantic runs through any manageable high-water rapids. Occasionally, boats swamped or capsized. Some were caught in whirlpools and thrown against rocks with terrible force. In camp, they did what they could to patch the withering planks. Nights were even more miserable, as they shivered in wet bedrolls. Their only sustenance came from coffee and dense flatbread—typically a first course to multipart breakfasts on modern river trips.

Bradley remained content as the expedition would allow his discharge from the army. For the opportunity, he expressed willingness to explore the River Styx. During those chaotic days in August, the Colorado may have seemed more harrowing than the placid river of death. Bradley vowed sweet revenge upon the first good food he could find. Mormon settlers had estimated the Grand Canyon to be 70 to 80 miles long, yet the expedition had already come down 150. How long could this misery last?

The next day, they reached a volcanic monument in the river, later called Vulcan's Anvil. This prompted Powell to make a longer journal entry, which had become increasingly clipped and rare. He noticed that basalt lava had previously flowed over the canyon rim and dammed the river before eroding. They portaged Lava Falls on left, the steepest rapid Sumner believed he'd seen on the trip.

Eventually, they entered what today is called Lower Granite Gorge. Bradley feared the worst, a return of bedrock-defined rapids. They found a Native American camp with two beddings sewn from wildcat skins and assumed the occupants were off hunting in the mountains. The men stole a dozen squash and some unripe melons and corn from a vegetable garden, wishing later they'd stolen more.

On August 27, the nine men reached the worst rapid yet, about 3 months and 950 miles down their route. The current dashed against river-left cliffs and was thrown back center into billows and crashing waves. Bradley feared the boats would either flip in the center waves or smash against rocks along the sides. The crew spent the rest of the day searching for a way around. In his 1875 account, Powell describes walking

Repairing a boat in upper Granite Gorge; J. K. Hillers, 1872. US GEOLOGICAL SURVEY

along a narrowing ledge on river-right. Hopping forward, he clutched a rock and realized he was unable to move forward or backward. He was "cliffed-out" 400 feet above the river. Powell called for help and waited as the men wedged oars around him to create a catwalk. Down to 5 days of rations, they camped above the rapid for the night.

After a meager supper, Oramel Howland asked to speak with Powell. The two walked up a little creek, where Oramel explained that he, his brother Seneca, and William Dunn had decided to go no farther. They'd take to the mountains come morning, walking north in the general direction of Mormon settlements. Howland suggested Powell and the others join. Powell and Howland returned to camp, saying nothing, but Bradley observed the discontent and correctly feared some of the party might leave. He called it the darkest day of the trip, but he was determined to stay on the river, run the rapid, and earn his discharge.

Powell had a restless night. First, he plotted their course over the past two harrowing days. Next, using his sextant, he took measurements of latitude and found the estimates in agreement. The mouth of the Virgin River, the nearest spot on the Colorado River to the Mormon settlements, was perhaps 45 miles in a straight line. That meant 80 to 90 miles on the meandering river. And the character of the river between the Grand Wash Cliffs and the Virgin was known to be flatwater for many miles. Powell woke Howland to share the belief they were nearly through Grand Canyon. Howland listened and went back to sleep. Then Powell went one by one to Walter, Hawkins, Sumner, Bradley, and Hall. Each agreed to continue.

The next morning, the mood was somber and the decisions firm. The three men would take their chances with 75 miles of open desert, certainly full of water pockets from all the rain. With rifles, ammunition, and some provisions, they hiked partway up the cliffs to watch the remaining six men descend the rapid. In his journal, Powell wrote only three words: "Boys left us." Bradley offered, "They left us with good feelings though we deeply regret their loss for they are as fine fellows as I ever had the good fortune to meet."

The pilot boat, *Emma Dean*, was abandoned. The six men divided into the two freight boats, each nearly empty by now. They crossed the river and carried around one bad point, then hopped in and plunged into what became Separation Rapids. They rowed with all their might into boils and billows until all they could do was hold on and hope. As Sumner described, they shipped half-full of water in a perfect hell of foam.

They came through upright, and not even an oar was lost. Powell claimed they fired pistols to signal the out-of-sight trio their success, waiting several hours on hopes they'd change their minds and come down in the *Emma Dean*. Sumner later claimed the three men were in sight the whole time and motioned for the boats to go onward before hiking away. Eventually, the six men in two boats continued downstream.

Lava Falls rushes past the camera of J. K. Hillers. US GEOLOGICAL SURVEY

Bradley claimed they'd never before run such a rapid, but later that afternoon they reached one even worse.

They arrived at a place where lava had hardened atop granite and large boulders created a slalom course from the river. Later called Lava Cliff Rapid, now flooded beneath Lake Mead, it would be considered one of the hardest rapids in Grand Canyon. To the men, it looked possible to line past beneath the cliffs. Bradley remained in the first boat to guide it down, while the remaining men clutched the bow rope and climbed the cliffs to let the boat down.

At first, this worked. The boat played down the cliff, with Bradley using an oar to push around rocks. But as the cliffs rose higher and the current quickened, the boat halted. They'd reached the end of the 120-foot rope. Bradley was fully under a ledge, out of sight from the men. The river roared furiously. Despite shouts on either end, neither party heard the other. On the cliff, a few men held the rope fast while others ran for a second rope.

Below, Bradley was in a bad spot; his boat bounced and bucked next to an outcrop of rock. If the rope were just 4 feet longer, Bradley believed he could swing into the eddy below. But as it was, any sharp tug or slackening of the rope might pendulum his boat into current and rocks. Bradley pulled out his knife while scanning the rapid below for a path through the foaming cataract. He wrote that it felt like his boat was a medieval torture rack and he the stretched victim.

Above, the men were tying the two ropes together. Below, Bradley felt a horrific tug, and his boat shot into the current. Next, a snap. The entire cutwater, the curved plank that reinforced the bow of each Whitehall rowboat and held the iron eyebolt attached to the rope, released from the boat. The cutwater flew through the air with the recoiling rope, and Bradley's boat dashed into the raging waves "like a war-horse eager for the fray."

Bradley was finally running a rapid of the size and force he'd pondered for months. Being the only rower and set of eyes in the boat demanded a new approach. He couldn't muscle through alone, backward and blind. The bow still faced upstream so Bradley dropped in an oar and yanked with all his might to turn the boat downstream. It seems possible that when he sat, he did so in the unoccupied second seat, facing forward. Bradley was likely aware of the accidental but successful stern-first descent in Split Mountain Canyon, described by Oramel Howland. So why wouldn't the expedition's most creative member and most adventurous rower face downstream when the circumstances demanded?

Bradley describes something remarkably similar to modern whitewater rowing, dropping in oars strategically on each side to guide the boat through the collection of waves, holes, and boulders. And if this supposition is true, that means George Bradley became America's prototype whitewater boater almost three decades before Nathaniel Galloway developed the modern technique on the very same rivers the expedition descended. Soon, Bradley passed the worst part of the rapid and emerged below, waving his hat triumphantly to the boys on the cliffs.

Above, the men had probably fallen against the cliffs as the rope went slack. Powell watched the cutwater fling through the air as Bradley turned into massive waves and disappeared in the maelstrom. The major later said that nothing ever gave him more joy than seeing Bradley make it through safely. Soon after, Powell and the second boat followed Bradley's lead into the rapid. They shipped half-full of water, spun around, and nearly collided with rocks, but otherwise made it through as well. Perhaps two moments of relief only matched the next morning when the six men in two boats exited the Grand Canyon at the Grand Wash Cliffs.

The 1869 adventure concludes on page 211 . . .

10

LOWER COLORADO RIVER AND RESERVOIRS

PLENTY OF POWELL PILGRIMS REACH DIAMOND CREEK or Pearce Ferry, pack up, and go home. Route complete, right? Well, that's close to true, what with the 1869 expedition officially ending at the mouth of Virgin River, now flooded under Lake Mead, and about a 43-mile paddle from Pearce. But for those who look downstream, many paddling opportunities exist. While the sections in this segment are quite different from the scenic canyons of the Colorado Plateau upstream, the lower Colorado River and reservoirs have their own unique charms and quirks.

Talk about a truly desolate region. The landscape is mostly volcanic in origin, with shades of black, brown, gray—occasionally with reddish and orange hues, if you're lucky—while sand dunes saunter about. Most people zip through this region on high speed highways and interstates in air-conditioned vehicles like in a scene from *Fahrenheit 451*. And it is very hot—peak summer highs almost average 110 degrees. Average! That means it sometimes reaches 120 or more. With a few exceptions, it's typically too hot to paddle here in the summer. And with all the reservoirs—Mead, Mohave, Havasu— and proximity to population centers, it's mostly a motors and speedboat scene from spring to fall.

Still, there are certain spots and times of year that allow for some excellent paddling trips. In this segment I've highlighted three options, but there are many more worth exploring. The remote Temple Bay on Lake Mead has a forgotten feel to it. The remarkable and popular Black Canyon of the Colorado below Hoover Dam—with more of a hot spring scene than solitude feel—is a fun "Vegas" of float streams, but a quota system at put-in limits overall numbers to a reasonable amount. Downstream, the angular Topock Gorge looks like an alien landscape, right down to the quarter-mil jet boats that race through the wildlife refuge. With no camping, a long day trip there in winter would be rewarding. Or there's a no-wake zone for paddling near the London Bridge on Lake Havasu. And many more options throughout the segment,

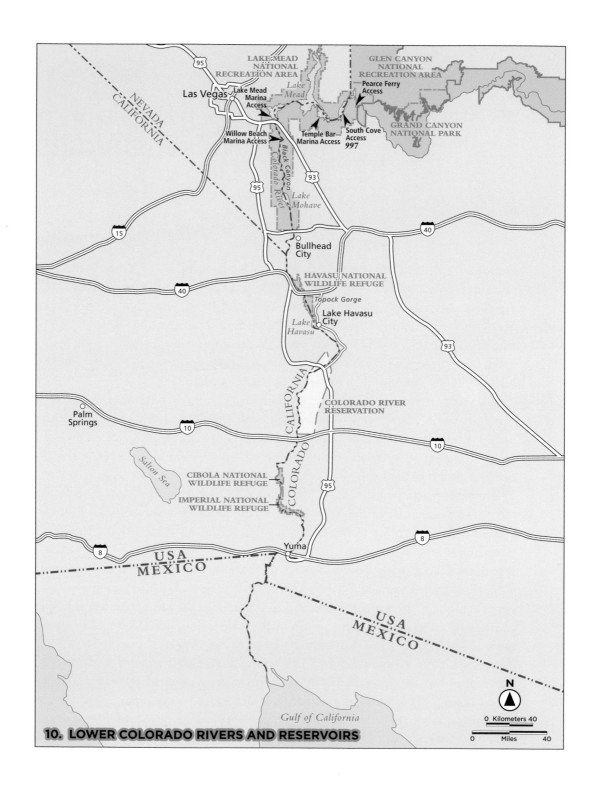

10. LOWER COLORADO RIVERS AND RESERVOIRS

"Where the Colorado River forms the boundary between California and Arizona it cuts through a number of volcanic rocks by black, yawning canyons." —John Wesley Powell

including downstream of Parker Dam. All told, the lower Colorado won't win any awards for best paddling along the Powell route, but it could take honorable mention for *worth it* opportunities in a mild winter region that paddlers live near or are passing through.

Season and weather: You can paddle the lower Colorado River and reservoir year round, but peak summer season is challenging due to high heat (over 100°F) and heavy motorboat traffic in certain sections. For that reason, the recommended paddling season tends to be mid-fall to early spring.

Water level and character: The Colorado River below Hoover Dam is all class I.

Outfitters and services: Desert River Outfitters, located in Bullhead City, runs many trips across the entire 400-mile segment, including Black Canyon, Topock, and more. They can assist through-paddlers or those curious about shorter options. (928) 763-3033; www.desertriveroutfitters.com.

Will Stauffer-Norris was born in Idaho, grew up in Virginia, and graduated from Colorado College in 2011. Before senior year, Will and Zak Podmore began the first of two source-to-sea expeditions on both the Green and Colorado Rivers. These days, Will combines passions for wild rivers, visual art, and adventure to document remote and beautiful places across the planet. His work has appeared at the Banff and 5Point film festivals and on the pages of *National Geographic*. He runs the Seattle-based virtual reality production company Imbue Reality.

Mike: What gave you the idea to go source-to-sea, and how did the project evolve along the way?

Will: I wanted to do the longest river trip possible! Zak and I had been on shorter river trips all around the western United States, and we were curious what a 3½-month river trip would be like. Along the way, we realized that seeing so much made us ambassadors for these rivers. That motivated us to share our experience through film, photography, writing, and public speaking.

Mike: The 3-minute time-lapse video from your first trip was great! [view at https://vimeo.com/60269562] How did that come together?

Will: That was a side experiment that turned out pretty cool. I took thirty frames of GoPro footage every day so a viewer could see the river change over its entire length. What's striking is the river gets bigger, as rivers tend to do, until after the Grand Canyon. Below Lake Mead, the river gets smaller and smaller, as diversions suck water out of the Colorado. Finally, the river becomes irrigation canals in Mexico, then it vanishes into desert. Most rivers don't ever get smaller. For me, that drives home the plight of the Colorado River.

Mike: What else did you learn on your expeditions?

Will: One realization was that despite the Green and Colorado being like one long and connected river, paddlers tend to divide them into distinct "river trips" based on the surrounding terrain. But there were so many sections, in between better-known canyons, that turned out to be really interesting. They may not have had dramatic canyon walls, but these open sections of river were thick with wildlife. On the Green in Wyoming, we saw moose around many corners. On the lower Colorado, we paddled through insane flocks of birds. Every section of the river has unique characteristics, and it's so remote for most of its length.

Mike: Did Powell figure in much during your trips?

Will: We both read Powell's book before the trip, plus Wallace Stegner's *Beyond the Hundredth Meridian*. Both are critical reading for anyone traveling through the American West. But we tried not to compare our trip to Powell's expeditions. With the benefit of iPhones, plastic kayaks, and friends along the way, it's much less of a feat to paddle these rivers when compared to Powell's first descent. The hardest things for us were negotiating the bureaucracy and paddling the reservoirs! I couldn't have made it across the reservoirs without Zak setting the pace.

Mike: What were some favorite lasting memories?

Will: Too many to list! I loved getting to the take-out of a certain section and we'd keep going! At some take-outs, friends had to go back to their normal lives, but we kept paddling. Another favorite was on the lower Colorado. We were tired, so we strapped our sea kayaks together, inflated our pack rafts, set those on top, and slept while floating. We woke up a few times when we hit bushes, but we made some serious downstream progress while lounging!

Mike: Any advice for paddlers considering a source-to-sea or other major through-trip?

Will: The hardest part was definitely Mexico, but by that point we'd come too far to stop. We couldn't get straight answers on which canals would have enough water to float. Access to drinking water was difficult because there isn't any nonpolluted water. We had a ton of help from friends at the nearby Sonoran Institute , and we couldn't have made it without them. Overall, I wish we had planned more rest days to go hiking, but we were on a pretty strict schedule due to permit dates. But there's also a beauty to steadily covering miles, day after day, and then looking at a map and realizing you've just paddled across an entire state. To any paddlers considering going source-to-sea, despite any challenges, it will be one of the wildest experiences of your life. Do it.

Zak Podmore paddles the lower Colorado River through Mexico on the way toward the Gulf of California. WILL STAUFFER-NORRIS

Taking a break during a day trip out of Temple Bar on Lake Mead. Looking west toward where the Powell expedition ended in 1869.

WACKO, or Western Arizona Canoe & Kayak Outfitters, offers paddling trips in the Lake Havasu area, including the reservoir, Topock, and Bill Williams Wildlife Refuge; (928) 855-6414; www.azwacko.com.

Boats: Any flatwater-capable boat will do, with touring or open/sit-on-top kayak, canoe, and increasingly SUP the most popular.

PADDLING: LAKE MEAD

There's nothing wrong with paddling here. (Look, Lake Mead, you're fine, okay. It's not you, it's us.) Compared to the impacted river and reservoirs below, Lake Mead has

Temple Butte rises to the left, while the Grand Wash Cliffs, which mark the end of the Grand Canyon, loom in the background to the right.

some advantages. It's a practically empty, wild, semideserted, semiforgotten reservoir. The Boulder Bay area, closest to Vegas, sees the most motorboat traffic. Paddlers looking for a remote corner of the reservoir to paddle should consider Temple Bay, which offers dramatic views of the Grand Wash Cliffs. To paddle the entire reservoir from Pearce Ferry to Boulder Bay, you're looking at about 60 miles of center-line paddling, more if following the shoreline.

Access: There are four main options, but just downstream of Pearce Ferry, there is currently a dangerous class V rapid that formed through deposited sediments as the reservoir level dropped. Thus, lake paddlers should focus on the other three: South

Cove boat ramp (N36 5.44' / W114 6.36'); Temple Bay Marina boat ramp (N36 2.40' / W114 18.97'); Lake Mead Marina—aka Boulder Bay—boat ramp (N36 1.82' / W114 46.50'). There is a boat ramp at Echo Bay, on the Virgin River arm, but the marina closed in 2013 due to lowering reservoir levels. You'll need to conduct supplementary research to determine accessibility.

Camping: Dispersed primitive camping is allowed anywhere in the backcountry of Lake Mead National Recreation Area. Follow leave-no-trace practices (see page xxx), except within 0.5 mile of roads and facilities.

Regulations, agencies, fees: Lake Mead National Recreation Area requires a vehicle entry fee or National Parks Pass: (702) 293-8990; www.nps.gov/lake. The state of Nevada requires an invasive species sticker for some nonmotorized watercraft (see page 11).

Maps: The Lake Mead NPS unit offers several decent maps at kiosks and visitor centers, or you can print from their website. *National Geographic* Waterproof Trails Illustrated #204: Lake Mead National Recreation Area.

Highlights: Temple Butte rises on the north shore across from Temple Bar Marina, both located about 14 center-line miles southwest from South Cove. • The now-flooded confluence of the Colorado and Virgin Rivers, which marks the official end of the 1869 expedition, is located in the middle of the eastern half of a wide bay, about 10 miles west of Temple Bay and about 1,000 paddling miles from Green River, WY. • For through-paddlers, to reach Lake Mead Marina in Boulder Bay is another 25 center-line miles to the west.

PADDLING: BLACK CANYON OF THE COLORADO

If you do only one river section from this segment, this would be a good choice. I call it the "Vegas of float streams" because it sees heavy but not always overwhelming visitation. It has great hot springs, scrambly side hikes, dam-related sites, scenic canyon views, and a feeling of constructed nature. Hey, some people like Vegas. This is a great section for family and friend trips and a great river for winter overnights! Paddlers seeking longer trips can continue to Lake Mohave but will need to perform supplementary research into access locations or work with an outfitter, like Desert River Outfitters.

Access: You'll need to join an outfitter for access to put-in just below Hoover Dam. The lower access is a gravel boat ramp at Willow Beach Marina (N35 52.18' / W114 39.64'). Note that some people paddle upstream from Willow Beach for day trips or overnights. If you time your paddling with lower releases, the current is mellower, and strong paddlers might even reach the dam.

In Black Canyon of the Colorado River, many paddlers float into Emerald Cave at mile 9.5, and then they don't much like to float out. WHIT RICHARDSON

Challenges and safety: The main point I'd like to raise is the water is very cold, so beginners should use a stable boat to avoid accidental swims.

Camping: Primitive camping is allowed anywhere following leave-no-trace principles (see page xxx), but many overnight paddlers go to Arizona Hot Springs for the pools, the pit toilet, and the "scene."

Supplies: Boulder City, NV, has plenty of stores and restaurants—bring your buffet pants.

Note: All other details are the same as the Lake Mead section above.

Highlights: There are too many to name, but keep an eye out for a bore hole drilled during dam construction that is now a sauna cave on river-right, 0.5 mile below launch. • At 0.25 mile below that, on river-right, is Gold Strike Canyon; a trail leads up to Nevada Hot Spring. • At mile 1.75 you'll find Boy Scout Canyon on river-right, with a hike to hot spring. • There are some interesting ring bolts at mile 3.5 on

Walking from one pool to the next at Arizona Hot Springs, which is on the Arizona side of the river, if that part wasn't clear.

river-left, where old steamboats were tied up. • At mile 3.75, on river-left, is Arizona Hot Springs—a popular camp with an outhouse and a mile hike to the biggest collection of hot springs in this section; it can get very crowded and become party central here during peak season and weekends. • At mile 9.5 Emerald Cave is on river-left. There's much more to discover down there.

PADDLING: TOPOCK GORGE AND LAKE HAVASU

The craggy volcanic pinnacles that rise with improbable geometry from the small mountains of Topock Gorge are one of the most startling sights along the lower Colorado River. The nearby town of Needles, CA, was named for these intrusive volcanic rocks. The water is cold and clear coming out of Davis Dam about 40 river miles

At Lake Havasu, more known for seminude spring breakers, semiclothed paddleboarding is exploding in popularity in no-wake zones.

upstream near Bullhead City, AZ. During high season, from around Mar to Oct, the area is filled with motorboats. There are heavily enforced speed restrictions for several miles in the inner gorge. But above and below, speedboats travel fast and create high wakes that could upset paddlers. For this reason, paddlers should consider visiting from Nov to Feb. While there was once a popular paddling scene at Topock and Havasu, the interest seems to have diminished in recent years.

Duration: The typical 1-day Topock trip is 14 miles from Topock Marina to Castle Rock. Much shorter out-and-back trips on the lake are possible using access points below or others listed on the refuge website.

Access: Start at Topock Marina in Arizona (N34 43.16' / W114 28.96') or Moabi Regional Park/Pirate Cove Resort in California (N34 43.72' / W114 30.67'). End at Castle Rock Bay Access (N34 33.95' / W114 23.55), Mesquite Bay Access (N34 30.80' / W114 22.09'), Havasu State Park at Windsor Beach (N34 29.54' / W114 21.63'), or other local access points.

Regulations, agencies, fees: Both starting marinas charge access fees. Havasu National Wildlife Refuge has a canoeing and kayaking page on its website, which lists access points and rules: www.fws.gov/refuge/Havasu/.

Challenges and safety: If you do paddle during high season, and possibly any time of year around popular Havasu, consider attaching a kayak safety flag, often orange flags on a pole 3–4 feet tall, to the stern of your boat. Motorboats use similar caution flags to indicate swimmers in the water or mechanical problems. Motorboat operators watch for these flags and are more likely to spot a low-lying kayak with one affixed.

OTHER PADDLING: LOWER COLORADO

There's so much more down there to explore, but I haven't seen it all myself. Yet. For now, I recommend Helen at Desert River Outfitters be your guide.

1869 EPILOGUE: AFTER THE EXPEDITION—PLUS, WHO WAS JWP?

Pig out, disband • a "side" trip to the gulf • fates of the ten • controversies deepen • welcome to head-spin eddy • farewell on your voyages!

Below Lava Cliff Rapid, the men ran all the diminishing rapids without scouting. The next day, they floated out from the Grand Wash Cliffs into a basin of low,

J. K. Hillers captures the view to the west from Toroweap overlook. US GEOLOGICAL SURVEY

rolling desert. With hopes that the worst was over, Bradley wrote, "All we regret now is that the three boys who took to the mountains are not here to share our joy and triumph."

Rowing onward, they entered a small valley and landed where a family of Native Americans had built a shelter from branches. Powell, who in 10 years would become the founding director of the US Bureau of American Ethnology, assured the frightened family that the six ragged white men were friendlies. Sumner made a few hypocritical and racist notes about the natives' hygiene, clothes, and shelter.

That evening, the men reached the mouth of the Virgin River, today buried beneath Lake Mead. Four people were fishing in the river, a white father, two adult sons, and a native boy. They'd heard about Powell's expedition. In fact, they'd read news that all had perished. They invited these half-starved phantoms to their cabin for all the fish and squash they could eat. And everyone—including Bradley, who had sworn an oath of overindulgence in a posttrip meal—happily complied.

The expedition had come over 1,000 river miles in just under 100 days. They'd seen some of the American West's most scenic river canyons. They'd run over 500 rapids of all sizes, portaging about a hundred of the worst. Lost two boats. Four men had departed along the way. They'd destroyed or lost thousands of dollars in equipment—which would be tens of thousands today. Of the scientific objectives, they'd accomplished none. There were more leftover dried apples than rock samples and fossils. Powell had only a roughly estimated map. A few crudely fixed points made a faint constellation across America's blank spot.

"After two years of hard work of exploration of the Colorado and its tributaries," wrote Sumner in his final journal entry, "I find myself penniless and disgusted with the whole thing, sitting under a mesquite bush in the sand." As the first expedition ended, it's unclear how much money Powell paid to his crew. Though most sources and historians agree Powell paid something to each man, it was probably far less than what was originally agreed upon and recorded in the few surviving contracts, a controversy that lingered, even festered, for some of the men in later years.

On the last day of August 1869, the first expedition disbanded. Sumner, along with Bradley, Hawkins, and Hall, received the two remaining freight boats from Powell, plus a small resupply of rations brought in from nearby Callville, NV. Their goal was to continue rowing south along the flat Colorado River through a volcanic landscape in known country. They started the next day, and only a few letters and later accounts record this post-expedition adventure.

Bradley and Hawkins seem to have floated as far as Ehrenberg, AZ, before going overland and splitting up. Of all ten on the first expedition, Hawkins lived the longest, until age 71. He died in Arizona in 1921, after a life of farming and ranching. Little is known of Bradley after the expedition. Historian Michael Ghiglieri found evidence that Bradley spent most of his life in California before a bad injury forced him to return to New England, where he soon died at age 50 in 1885. Thirty years later, a nephew found Bradley's lively journal from the expedition and offered it to the Library of Congress.

Sumner and Hall continued downriver all the way to the Gulf of California. Supposedly, like true mountain men, they floated around the barren rocky landscape for a few skeptical hours. Disappointed

Tau-gu, chief of the Paiutes, overlooking the Virgin River with John Wesley Powell when the major was 39 years old. NATIONAL PARK SERVICE

at the prospects and flat broke, they rigged a sheet from a covered wagon as a sail and went right back up the river to Fort Yuma. Sadly, Hall, the youngest member of the expedition, died first. He was murdered at 32 years old, shot in the back by robbers while working security for an Arizona mail route. Sumner was a wild card until the end, his final journal entry reading, "I shoulder my gun and bidding all adieu I go again to the wilderness." He rambled across the West, raising a family in Denver, placer gold mining in Glen Canyon, and dying in the Uinta Basin at age 67 in 1907. Nearby, Frank Goodman had settled to raise a big family in Vernal, where some have pondered if his tales of disaster in Lodore could have inspired Nathaniel Galloway to revolutionize whitewater rowing.

By September 1, 1869, John Wesley and brother, Walter, were traveling overland to Salt Lake City with a plan to take a train east. Along the way, they asked the Mormon settlers to watch for Dunn and the two Howland brothers. But on September 8, word came from a newspaper article and telegram that the three men were dead, allegedly murdered by members of the Shivwits tribe in retaliation for the killing of a native woman. Powell doubted the three had murdered anyone, but he accepted the accounts of their murder by the Shivwits as a misunderstanding. No bodies were ever found, no direct evidence offered—only hearsay. So, historians accepted this story for over 100 years.

That accepted story became disputed by original expedition members, particularly later in their lives. Eventually, many revisionist historians claimed the three had been killed by Mormon militia members. Perhaps a robbery? Perhaps mistaking them as American spies? The latter theory relates to the same fear of outsiders that had prompted the Mountain Meadows Massacre in 1857. The only participant charged and eventually executed for that massacre—the investigation of which was postponed due to the Civil War—was John D. Lee. He started a ferry service—using the *Nellie Powell*, a boat abandoned by the second expedition—where river runners today launch on Grand Canyon trips. At this point, we're definitely beyond the scope of this book. For those interested in descending the whirlpool of Powell route history, please return to the resources section, pick up everything, put it in a boat—and don't forget croakies for a dozen pairs of reading glasses.

By September 18, Powell was crossing the continent, perhaps already dreaming up ambitious plans as he sped over the bridge near where they'd started 4 months before. Within a year, he would return to the route to begin preparations for another, more deliberate mapping expedition. This second expedition was fully funded by the US government, launching from Green River Station on May 22, 1871. A new crew was selected more for scientific expertise than mountain man abilities. Powell added sweep oars to slightly updated rowboats. They brought two giant cameras, though the photographers kept quitting. The crew didn't destroy any boats, but otherwise the

John Wesley Powell's lashed armchair in Marble Canyon. J. K. Hillers. US GEOLOGICAL SURVEY

usual chaos of portages and swims returned. There was another fire in camp. This time everyone had lifejackets, not just Powell. At one point they bailed their boats with a tea kettle and eventually their hats. Due to high water in July 1872, a dwindling crew of seven hiked out of the Grand Canyon at Kanab Creek.

On the second expedition was a remarkable, if impressionable, young man who for the rest of his life would idolize Powell, even while acknowledging his faults. This 17-year-old, Frederick Dellenbaugh, later wrote *A Canyon Voyage*, the best book written by anyone on either expedition. The most important member was Powell's brother-in-law, Almon Harris Thompson, who did all the work. Among other things, "Prof" organized the mapping and led a remarkable overland expedition to the Escalante River, the last major river mapped by white Americans.

Powell's career progressed. He always seemed to be moving from one idea to the next. He went on the lecture circuit, telling the tale of his 1869 expedition and the daring men who kept saving his life. In 1874, he founded the Cosmos Club, and in 1879, the Bureau of Ethnology, which recorded and catalogued Native American culture during

Isn't it great when a tree offers perfect symbolism behind a 70-year-old monument? Expedition Island, Green River, WY. US Geological Survey

periods of extermination and confinement. In 1881, he became the second director of the US Geological Survey. In the 1890s, Powell even took a crack at writing nearly undecipherable philosophy—it's possible only Wallace Stegner ever read it.

Powell was an idea guy, and at times it seems he left behind or forgot people who'd helped him progress at each step. In 1875, he finally published an account of his explorations of the Green and Colorado Rivers. But he did so by relaying the adventure of 1869 and inserting the scientific discoveries from 1871–72. The result is typically described as a semifictional work of literature. Powell heaped praise on the mountain men but entirely omitted the second crew. This offended Thompson, who wrote to Dellenbaugh, "Everything we know about the Colorado River except the fact that it could be passed down in boats was secured by the second voyage and subsequent explorations." And yet Powell, in a letter, encouraged Dellenbaugh to tell the story of the second expedition. At this point, a Powell pilgrim's head is likely spinning in an eddy.

We've reached our final mile. The take-out is up ahead. There's *so* much left to share, but the editors have given the eddy-out signal. So, who was John Wesley Powell? I wish I knew. After 5 years exploring the route and researching the expeditions, I find myself more unsure than ever. Few answers, many clues, more questions. Powell, in the same conversations, is called a prophet, a visionary, a politician, a jerk (I've heard far worse, actually), an adventurer, a scientist, a river runner, a fraud. He was certainly an explorer. And he left a complicated legacy with much left to discover.

I remain curious about Powell, and I plan to learn more. But at this point, I'm not sure I care who Powell was as a person, exactly. Ours is a revisionist age, where it seems everyone is in a rush to take sides regarding historic figures. To recruit these often mercurial phantoms to our own "side" in an argument. To appropriate these faint portrayals to push certain political agendas. It seems Powell constructed and convoluted his own image just enough to allow for such widely different interpretations. Instead of judging, we could just ask, "What can we each learn from the story?"

I do know this. The John Wesley Powell route is one of those rare places, where 150 years later, the trips still come to life with much of the drama and vitality of the ten men in wooden rowboats who explored there in 1869. It lives in the pages of journals and retellings. It lives in canyons and rapids and reservoirs where a one-armed Civil War major, some ragtag mountain men, a few traumatized ex-soldiers, and a slew of wannabe scientists dreamed up a ridiculous idea to fumble down a pair of rivers for a thousand miles through harsh desert and make a map. Then they did it. Twice. And stumbled into history books, flaws and all. Maybe no pilgrimage along the Powell route ever feels complete? Mine feels like it's still beginning. Each trip is a grand revisitation, floating through river canyons like turning pages in a book. Heck yeah, we can read it over and over again. I hope to see you out there.

About the Author

Mike Bezemek is the author and photographer of books, blogs, and articles for a variety of publications, including the guidebook *Paddling the Ozarks* for FalconGuides. As a contributing editor for *Canoe & Kayak* magazine, he writes two recurring series—"Weekend Expeditions" and "Regular Paddler, Remarkable Waters." Other projects include a bikepacking article series for *Adventure Cyclist* magazine and a satirical review series about "shitty" beer that is currently seeking a new home. *Twit Lit Classics*, for Skyhorse Publishing, is a humorous literature companion book series that reimagines classic works of adventure literature as Twitter feeds. And his blog, Hot Mess of an Adventure Writer Tells All: Confessions, Lessons, and Mishaps from the Field, can be found at hotmessadventure.com. View his work or contact him at mikebezemek.com.